AI & HUMAN INSIGHT
FOR EDUCATIONAL LANDSCAPE

ABOUT THE EDITORS

Dr. Pooja Gupta currently serving as an Associate Professor at the School of Liberal Arts, IILM University, India. She holds a Ph.D. in English Literature and Language, and brings over 16 years of diverse experience in teaching, research, and academic leadership. Dr. Gupta has chaired eight international conferences, delivered keynote addresses, and presented more than 18 research papers at national and international platforms. Her scholarly contributions include 15 peer-reviewed journal publications and five books published by both national and international publishers.

Dr. Pooja Batra Nagpal currently working as an Associate Professor in Computer Science Department in IILM University Gurugram, Haryana, India. She has experience of teaching in Amity University, Gurgaon. She has collaborated with various MNC clients like FirstRain, Codegems solution, Crossover, Fractal, IBM, Phemesoft, Magnus Corporation, Revanza Impex International and organizations like Kurukshetra University, Bharat Group of Institutions, Indraprastha Group of Institutions, Venkateswara University and others. She has published more than 40 research papers in reputed and indexed journals, published many patents and books, presented papers in international conference. Received many awards including women scientist award by govt organisation.

AI & HUMAN INSIGHT
FOR EDUCATIONAL LANDSCAPE

Dr. Pooja Gupta

Dr. Pooja Batra Nagpal

ACADEMIC ENCLAVE

First Edition, 2025

ISBN: 978-93-48642-80-6

Published by
ACADEMIC ENCLAVE™
House No. 10/15, Ground Floor,
Block-A, Street No. 14/3, Kamal Vihar,
Kamal Pur, Burari, Delhi-110084
Email: info@academicenclave.com
Mobile: +91-7042423166
Website: www.academicenclave.com

Printed at Replika Press Pvt. Ltd.

Preface

The intersection of Artificial Intelligence (AI) and Education marks a significant paradigm shift in the evolution of human knowledge, interaction, and institutional governance. As we navigate the fourth industrial revolution, the application of AI within educational ecosystems is not merely an innovation—it is a transformation that challenges traditional pedagogy, operational practices, and the very nature of cognitive development. It is within this context that the present volume, *AI and Human Insight for Educational Landscape*, has been conceived and compiled.

This book emerges from a growing recognition that while AI technologies are increasingly being integrated into educational platforms and strategies, the human dimension remains essential to their ethical and effective deployment. The contributions to this volume reflect a multidisciplinary engagement with AI's potential and pitfalls. They span legal, economic, psychological, pedagogical, and administrative dimensions—each chapter offering a unique perspective, grounded in research, reflective practice, and future-oriented thinking.

The opening chapter, *"Laws and Ethical Considerations for AI Usage in Generating Intellect,"* authored by Suresh Jaunsari, sets a foundational tone by addressing the ethical imperatives and legal frameworks necessary for responsible AI integration. This chapter foregrounds the importance of accountability, transparency, and human rights in the deployment of AI systems within educational contexts.

In the second chapter, *"Economic Analysis of AI Application in Education: An Overview,"* co-authors Sanskriti Bisht and Rishabh Kumar Tiwari offer a timely evaluation of the financial implications associated with AI adoption in educational institutions. Their discussion provides a robust framework for understanding cost structures, return on investment, and the scalability of AI solutions—issues of paramount concern for policymakers and institutional leaders alike.

Akshay Garg's contribution, *"Generative AI and Its Feasibility in the Developing Era: Opportunities, Challenges, and Strategic Pathways for Sustainable Development,"* navigates the complexities of AI implementation in emerging economies providing strategic pathways for leveraging AI to foster inclusive educational growth and reduce systemic inequities.

In *"Revolutionizing Psychology Training with the Help of Artificial Intelligence,"* Neha Kaushik explores how AI can enhance teaching methodologies and student engagement in psychology education. The chapter offers concrete examples of how simulation, intelligent feedback systems, and adaptive learning platforms can support both educators and learners in this highly nuanced field.

Divya Khatwani's chapter, *"Smart Pedagogy: Harnessing AI for Financial Learning,"* examines the intersection of financial literacy and digital pedagogy. Her research highlights the use of AI-driven tools to personalize financial education, making complex economic concepts more accessible, engaging, and contextually relevant.

The final chapter, *"The Role of Human Resources in Fostering Effective Mediation and Negotiation Processes,"* by Simran Kaur, draws attention to the pivotal role of human resource professionals in supporting AI-mediated communication and conflict resolution. Her work reaffirms the necessity of human facilitation in AI-augmented environments, emphasizing emotional intelligence, cultural sensitivity, and institutional cohesion.

Collectively, all the chapters in this volume reflect a confluence of scholarship, vision, and practical orientation. The contributors have approached their topics with both analytical rigor and a profound awareness of the real-world challenges and possibilities presented by AI in education to support the creation of an educational ecosystem that is more inclusive, efficient, ethical, and future-ready.

I extend my sincere appreciation to each of the contributors for their scholarly commitment, and to the institutions that have supported this endeavor. Their collective expertise has made this volume a meaningful contribution to contemporary educational discourse. I extend my thanks to the institution IILM University Gurugram for fostering such a congenial research oriented environment and supporting us throughout in academic endeavors.

It is our hope that this book will serve as a valuable resource for educators, researchers, technologists, and policymakers who are committed to understanding and shaping the future of education. May it encourage further inquiry, inform responsible practice, and inspire the thoughtful integration of artificial intelligence in service of human learning and development.

Dr. Pooja Gupta

Dr. Pooja Batra Nagpal

Contents

1

Laws and Ethical Considerations for AI Usage in Generating Intellect

Mr. Suresh
HNB University Srinagar Garhwal.
Email: sureshjaunsari@gmail.com

ABSTRACT

Artificial Intelligence (AI) has emerged as a transformative force, reshaping industries, economies, and societies. Among its applications, the generation of intellectual content has raised significant legal and ethical challenges. This paper examines the existing laws and ethical principles guiding AI's use in generating intellectual works. It analyzes key global frameworks, highlights gaps, and proposes a comprehensive approach to address issues such as authorship, accountability, bias, and societal impact. By integrating theoretical perspectives and real-world cases, the study offers actionable recommendations for fostering a responsible AI ecosystem.

Keywords

Artificial Intelligence, Ethics, Intellectual Property, Copyright, Accountability, Bias, Legal Frameworks, Societal Impact

Introduction

The ability of AI systems to generate intellectual content, ranging from text to music and art, is revolutionizing creativity and innovation. Tools like OpenAI'sChatGPT, DALL-E, and similar platforms are not only enhancing productivity but also challenging conventional notions of authorship, intellectual property, and ethical accountability. As these technologies proliferate, stakeholders face dilemmas about legal ownership, ethical use, and the societal consequences of deploying such systems.

This paper delves into these challenges, aiming to establish a coherent understanding of the laws and ethical considerations surrounding AI's role in generating intellect. It seeks to bridge the gaps between technological advancement, ethical responsibility, and legal frameworks.

Research Questions

- What are the existing laws governing AI-generated intellectual content?
- How do ethical considerations shape the development and deployment of AI systems?
- What gaps exist in current legal and ethical frameworks for AI-generated content?
- How can these gaps be addressed to ensure responsible AI usage?

Objectives

- To analyze global legal frameworks related to AI-generated intellectual property.
- To evaluate ethical principles guiding AI development and deployment.
- To identify gaps and inconsistencies in current laws and ethics.
- To propose recommendations for harmonizing legal and ethical approaches.

Theoretical Framework

The study draws on the following theoretical foundations:

- **Deontological Ethics**: Focuses on the duties and principles guiding AI creators and users, emphasizing transparency and fairness.
- **Consequentialism**: Evaluates the societal impacts of AI-generated content, including potential harm or benefit.
- **Legal Positivism**: Examines how existing laws apply to AI-generated content and the need for new legal constructs.
- **Socio-Technical Systems Theory**: Explores the interaction between AI technologies, legal systems, and societal values.

Methodology

This paper employs a qualitative research approach, combining:

- **Literature Review**: Analysis of academic papers, legal documents, and ethical guidelines.
- **Case Studies**: Examination of legal disputes and ethical controversies involving AI-generated content.
- **Comparative Analysis**: Evaluation of legal and ethical frameworks across different jurisdictions.
- **Expert Opinion**: Insights from legal scholars, ethicists, and AI practitioners.

Literature Review

Within academic and policy circles, there has been a substantial amount of discussion about the legal and ethical concerns that are associated with the use of artificial intelligence (AI) in the generation of intellectual output. Researchers have attacked the problem from a variety of angles, including rules pertaining to intellectual property, methods for reducing prejudice, ethical responsibility, and the effects on society. This section provides a synthesis of the current body of information in order to highlight the potential and problems that are provided by artificial intelligence technology in this particular area.

Within the realm of artificial intelligence-generated material, one of the most problematic elements is the subject of intellectual property (IP) rules. The fact that copyright rules have traditionally been draughted with human authorship in mind results in the existence of legal issues when it comes to dealing with work that is produced by artificial intelligence systems. The United States Copyright Office, for instance, makes it clear that it does not provide copyright protection to writers who are not human, which contributes to the perception that rules governing intellectual property are fundamentally anthropocentric (U.S. Copyright Office, 2022). In a similar vein, the case of Thaler v. Commissioner of Patents (2022) brought to light the unwillingness of courts in countries such as the United Kingdom and Australia to extend patent protection to artificial intelligence systems. In light of these incidents, it is clear that intellectual property rules need to be re-examined in order to take into account the collaborative and autonomous roles that AI plays in the production of material. On the other hand, several regimes, such as China, have taken a more pragmatic approach by giving copyright to the human being that controls the artificial intelligence system. This allows them to avoid the uncertain nature of authorship while still maintaining responsibility.

The Artificial Intelligence Act (2021) of the European Union is a noteworthy project that aims to regulate artificial intelligence systems. This act belongs to the category of global legal frameworks. Additionally, the Act does not adequately address the issues that are created by artificial intelligence in terms of the generation of intellectual material, despite the fact that its primary emphasis is on guaranteeing openness and accountability in applications of AI. The absence of clear legal rules that are adapted to the particular subtleties of works created by artificial intelligence in countries such as India and Japan is another factor that contributes to inconsistencies and gaps in global governance. Because of this fragmentation, it is more important than ever to develop worldwide legal standards that are harmonised, potentially under the auspices of organisations such as the World Intellectual Property Organisation (WIPO).

The issues of bias and fairness in artificial intelligence models have surfaced as major considerations from an ethical point of view. According to Floridi and Cowls (2019), artificial intelligence systems acquire biases that are incorporated in their training datasets. These biases have the potential to perpetuate discrimin and inequality. When it comes to recruiting algorithms, for instance, it has been shown that AI-powered algorithms tend to favour male applicants owing to previous biases in employment data. These kinds of biases not only give rise to ethical concerns, but they also provide organisations that use these technologies with potential legal vulnerabilities. Ethical standards, such as those recommended in the guidelines on automated decision-making that were developed by the European Commission in 2020, argue for more openness and inclusiveness in artificial intelligence systems in order to reduce the dangers that are associated with them.

Both accountability and transparency are recurrent topics in the ethical discussion around artificial intelligence. It is difficult to comprehend or describe the decision-making processes of many artificial intelligence systems due to the "black box" nature of these algorithms. The absence of transparency not only affects the confidence that users have in artificial intelligence systems, but it also makes it more difficult to assign culpability when such systems create outputs that are damaging or deceptive. The General Data Protection Regulation (GDPR) in the European Union is one example of a regulatory framework that places an emphasis on the need of explainability in artificial intelligence systems. This framework serves as a model for other countries to follow.

As the capabilities of AI technologies continue to advance, the problem of abuse and the spread of false information has become an increasingly pressing concern. Significant ethical challenges are presented by the fact that artificial intelligence systems are capable of producing deepfakes and other types of false material. As an example, artificial intelligence has been used to produce false information in order to sway public opinion during elections, so weakening democratic processes. For the purpose of preventing the inappropriate use of artificial intelligence technology, academics such as Whittaker et al. (2021) emphasise the need of ethical principles and technological safeguards.

The influence that artificial intelligence will have on creative processes and the structures of society and the economy is another area of worry. The widespread use of artificial intelligence systems like as DALL-E and ChatGPT raises doubts about the value of human creativity, despite the fact that these systems are capable of creating creative works that are on par with those produced by humans. In addition, the incorporation of artificial intelligence into creative sectors has resulted in concerns over the loss of jobs, especially in positions that are dependent on the production of content. It is imperative that ethical frameworks take into account these socio-economic ramifications in order to guarantee that the advantages of artificial intelligence are dispersed fairly across society. UNESCO (2021) emphasises the significance of bridging the digital divide in order to avoid underserved groups from depriving themselves of the advantages that artificial intelligence technology may provide.

Despite these advancements, there is still a large research deficit in the area of incorporating views from a variety of stakeholders into the governance of artificial intelligence. Existing frameworks are mostly moulded by viewpoints from countries that are technologically advanced, which may not effectively represent the requirements and values of areas that are still in the process of developing. By way of illustration, artificial intelligence (AI) legislation in

Europe and North America places an emphasis on transparency and justice, whilst in underdeveloped nations, access and cost may be prioritised. For this gap to be addressed, policymakers has to adopt a more inclusive approach, one that is informed by research that spans other cultures and other disciplines.

However, despite the fact that the legal and ethical concerns posed by artificial intelligence have been extensively reported, the convergence of these issues with socio-economic policy has not yet been thoroughly investigated. To democratise access to these technologies, for instance, policies that provide financial assistance to impoverished populations in order to purchase artificial intelligence equipment might play a significant role. On the other hand, discussions of such projects occurring within the context of ethical AI frameworks are uncommon, which highlights yet another topic that requires more investigation.

It may be concluded that the corpus of literature demonstrates a substantial amount of work on the legal and ethical aspects of material created by artificial intelligence, but it also highlights the need of adopting an approach that is more integrated and inclusive. Through the process of addressing gaps in global legal standards, ethical responsibility, and socio-economic policies, academics and policymakers have the opportunity to establish more solid frameworks for the responsible governance of artificial intelligence technology.

Research Gap

While significant progress has been made in understanding AI's capabilities and risks, the following gaps persist:

- Lack of harmonized global legal standards for AI-generated content.
- Limited focus on ethical accountability beyond technical bias.
- Insufficient integration of diverse stakeholder perspectives in AI governance.
- Neglect of socio-economic implications, particularly in developing regions.

Discussion

The intricacies of intellectual material that is created by artificial intelligence provide a myriad of issues that call for sophisticated considerations at the legal and ethical levels. At the heart of the issue is the uncertainty that exists about ownership of works created by artificial intelligence. Conventional legal frameworks have a difficult time adapting to situations that include non-human authorship. Legal ambiguity arises as a result of the lack of clarity over who owns the artificial intelligence product: the person who developed it, the person who uses it, or the entity that controls the system. In decisions such as Thaler v. Commissioner of Patents (2022), the courts have shown their ability.

Legal Challenges

Ambiguity in Ownership:

- Current laws fail to address whether AI, developers, or users own generated content.
- Example: A graphic design company using AI-generated logos faces uncertainty in claiming intellectual property rights.

Liability for Harmful Outputs:

- AI-generated misinformation or defamatory content lacks clear accountability mechanisms.
- Developers often disclaim responsibility, leaving users vulnerable.

Ethical Dilemmas

Bias in AI Models:

- Training datasets often lack diversity, leading to systemic biases in generated outputs.
- Regular audits and inclusive datasets are essential to mitigate this.

Impact on Human Creativity:

- As AI systems outperform humans in generating content, the value of human creativity diminishes.
- Ethical frameworks should balance innovation with protecting creators' rights.

Digital Divide:

- Access to AI tools remains unequal, exacerbating socio-economic disparities.

Proposals for Harmonization

Legal Reforms:

- Introduce AI-specific intellectual property laws recognizing human-AI collaboration.
- Establish international guidelines through bodies like WIPO.

Ethical Frameworks:

- Mandate transparency and explainability in AI systems.
- Develop standardized ethical audit protocols.

Socio-Economic Policies:

- Subsidize AI tools for underprivileged communities to bridge the digital divide.
- Encourage policies that foster equitable access to AI technologies.

Conclusion

AI's potential to generate intellect is transformative yet fraught with ethical and legal challenges. Addressing these requires a multidisciplinary approach integrating robust legal frameworks, ethical principles, and socio-economic policies. By fostering collaboration among stakeholders and prioritizing transparency, accountability, and inclusivity, societies can harness AI's benefits while mitigating risks.

Recommendations

1. Policy Development:

- Draft global AI-specific intellectual property laws.
- Encourage governments to adopt ethical AI principles.

2. Ethical AI Design:

- Promote transparency and accountability through regulatory mandates.
- Incorporate diverse perspectives in AI development.

3. Research Initiatives:

- Study the long-term impacts of AI on creative industries.

- Develop standardized metrics to evaluate ethical adherence.

References

- European Union. (2021). *Artificial Intelligence Act.* Retrieved from https://eur-lex.europa.eu
- U.S. Copyright Office. (2022). *Copyright Registration for AI Works.* Washington, DC.
- Thaler v. Commissioner of Patents. (2022). Federal Court of Australia.
- Floridi, L., & Cowls, J. (2019). The ethics of AI: Principles, challenges, and opportunities. *Oxford Internet Institute.*
- European Commission. (2020). *Guidelines on Automated Decision-Making*. Retrieved from https://ec.europa.eu
- Google AI Principles. (2018). *Responsible AI Development.* Mountain View, CA: Google.
- UNESCO. (2021). *AI and the Digital Divide*. Paris: UNESCO.
- OpenAI. (2023). *GPT and Ethical AI Design*. San Francisco, CA.

2

Economic Analysis of AI Application in Education: An Overview

Sanskriti Bisht[1] & Rishabh Kumar Tiwari[2]

(Doon University)

ABSTRACT

The integration of AI in education has present challenges and this study explores the transformative potential of AI in education and its broader economic implication. AI enhances education by personalizing learning, improving student performance and streamlining administrative tasks for institutions.. AI has the ability to modify learning models for each student based on their strengths and weaknesses. However, the challenges exist, part, particularly in developing economies, where AI integration exacerbate existing inequalities and may require significant policy adjustments. This highlights the standing of foreign investment in creating economic growth and ensuring equity is maintained (Zhai, Complexity, 2021).

This study aims to address existing knowledge gaps by exploring the financial implications of integrating AI into education, this study seeks to close current knowledge gaps. It will examine how economic growth , develop actionable strategies which will affect AI- powered education and evaluate the long term effect. The goal of this study is to suggest insightful information to educators who want to enhance AI results and promote long term economic growth.

This research investigates something that seems absent from existing literature; the economic consequences of inequality in learning opportunities arising from the integration of AI technologies, the frameworks for policies and funding which facilitate the mass uptake of AI within underdeveloped markets, and the macroeconomic consequences of having an AI generated educated workforce. These are evaluated qualitatively and quantitatively through the proposed mixed methods research design which was further triangulated with policy and funding review and multiple case studies from across the globe highlighting AI use in different socioeconomic contexts (Suvrat Jain and Dr. Roshita Jain, 2021).

The fundamental issue this paper investigates if there is an optimism bias regarding the role and future of AI, some secular trends do lend weight to the argument but they do also indicate a great possibility of increasing inequality and disempowerment of poorer strata of the society, all geographical areas will not be able to benefit. As the analysis makes clear, if the rapid advances being made in the AI field are not well governed, they will make chronic social inequalities worse, and this starkly highlights the urgency of timely policy response and the necessity of international collaboration towards systemic issues (Suvrat Jain and Dr. Roshita Jain, 2021).

To ensure that everyone can benefit from AI, policymakers need to focus on distributing AI technologies fairly. This includes investing in infrastructure and creating ethical guidelines. Such initiatives are crucial for improving the future workforce's quality and fostering innovation, which ultimately supports the overarching goal of providing equal attention and opportunities in education. (Zhai, Complexity, 2021).

Keywords: *AI- bidding for education services, Economic inequality, Legislative frameworks, Cost benefit assessment, Equipping the workforce*

1. Introduction

The swift development of Artificial Intelligence has greatly altered several sectors, one of which is the education sector too. Its application within the education sector has been considered to be revolutionary as sentient technologies possess new means that can transform the pedagogical process. This technology allows for greater efficiency by automating a variety of administrative activities and tailoring learning experiences to the particular interests of each student. Such changes indicate a great transformation of educational institutions whereby students may have better quality education, better curricula, and better educational outcomes. New technologies such as intelligent tutoring systems, machine learning, and natural language processing are beginning to disrupt the traditional teacher and student interaction and give rise to a new order of things that have many new ways of learning. However, the economic integration of AI into the education systems is a key issue that is complex in nature and inadequately tackled. This integration goes beyond technology integration and relates to the intersections of economics, equity, and policy.

Moreover, while there is a lot of talk on the use of AI in education with respect to creative and effective ways of teaching there hasn't been enough emphasis on the other side of the equation. What do you think are the economic consequences for higher productivity levels, job opportunities and economic growth by leveraging AI education. As the world is trying to transition to an AI Integrated education system, there are many questions which arise and need to be resolved. For instance, how will the AI enriched education system affect the job and the economies and the GDP in general?

The purpose of this study is to fill the gap in the current body of knowledge to support and see the scope of technological adoption in education with a focus on the economic implications. Three broad questions underlie the study: 1) The economic impact of AI in education in the context of learning inequalities and the degree wherein technology could potentially help to solve such inequalities, 2) The sources of policy and finance necessary for the large integration of AI into education systems, and 3) The effect of AI trained education on productivity, innovation and broader economic growth. Given this evaluation, the research intends to provide guidance to policymakers, educators, and economists who genuinely seek to build and use AI tools in the most optimal way, especially in the context of wider equity and sustainability on a global scale. As it becomes obvious that AI technologies continue advancing, the issue of their application in education becomes relevant in regard to social economic and policy effects stemming from the introduction of AI into the frameworks of educational systems. The intention of this study is to provide in great detail what the economic aspects will be that will guide the use of AI in educational systems so that such a transition is fair and beneficial across the globe. By carrying out deep analysis of contemporary literature and interrogating relevant policy documents, this paper seeks to provide the trajectory towards responsible use of AI in education as a way of mitigating the technology gap while promoting economic development of the spectrum of people.

2. Literature Review

2.1. AI and Socioeconomic Gaps in The Educational Sector

There is no doubt that AI will provide the opportunity for the education system to build a system of a more personalized approach for each of the students, however, there is also a growing concern as it has been noted in some research works regarding the blend of AI and education which can worsen the situation.

More specifically, disparities in AI access across different social classes are likely to sharpen the existing gap in education that separates the rich from the poor. What poor regions suffer from—lack of facilities, poor internet access, and the lack of properly trained teachers—hinders the equitable distribution of education supplemented with AI technologies. Therefore, as pointed out by Zhai (2021) and Jain & Jain (2021), these inequalities in the systems may restrict the extent even to which social mobility can happen leading to perpetuity of impoverished conditions. Hence, the potential technology that AI can hopefully offer to education may still be out of reach for myriad of multi-dimensional lowincome settings leaving its fair implications there on as far as equality in learning is concerned.

2.2. Policies and Funding for AI in Education Investing

Policies and Funding for AI in Education Investing in educational tools such as artificial intelligence (AI) requires efforts through both the public and private sectors. Collaboration among the society, entrepreneurs, and political actors becomes very important in ensuring the effectiveness of the AI with 3 respect to learning benefits. However, as Jain and Jain (2021) point out, having stimuli and endorsing policies are not enough, and over a long term, it is crucial to come up with sustainable funding mechanisms. Very often, the infrastructure and the resources required are never available due to the funding problems that are experienced. In other words, it is overly optimistic to expect AI to improve learning outcomes without thinking about how it will be funded. It has been established that without developing comprehensive policies, it is unlikely that the challenges will be solved effectively.

2.3. Impacts of AI in Education on the Broader Economy

AI is predicted to integrate into the education system and encourage growth, development, and emergence of new ideas which would positively impact the economy. Adoption AI in the education sector will yield a good quality workforce that is highly employable which in turn will increase the employment rate as well as increase the economic output. Still, there are disparities in the economic benefits brought forth the educational reform as pointed out by Zhai (2021). Developed economies that have embraced technology will reap the gains of the reforms faster compared to developing economies. In this regard, developing economies are likely to experience long lead times because of the existing barriers such as infrastructure, other investment related issues, as well as the people readiness and organizational structures to adopt the changes.

3. Research Objectives

This research has some basic areas, which is what has been defined. First, it will be estimated the economic effects of artificial intelligence in education sector targeting particularly social disparity area or those associated with differences in social classes.

Secondly, the research will help to formulate policy recommendations which aim at enabling funding to maintain the use of AI tools within education institutions. Thirdly, from the macroeconomic standpoint, we will evaluate how an AI ready workforce contributes to enhanced productivity, foster innovation, and promotes sustainable economic growth.

4. Methodology

The approach used in this study are based on prior research on the use of AI in classroom. We used a mixed method approach in this study, which allowed us to also use qualitative analysis to explore our research concerns. To begin, the study proposes and will conduct qualitative analysis through semistructured interviews with twenty different stakeholders in the educational sector, regarding their perspectives on social media, marketing and the implementation of marketing on an educational institution. The aim of this qualitative analysis is to better understand the socio-economic impacts of AI tools on users and providers in the education industry. Secondly, a policy analysis would be conducted on other countries as well to determine the possible gap and the existing scope for policy improvement that would use AI tools in the educational market and conference industry. This would aid in shaping the future policies as well.

5. Analysis derivative from some case studies

5.1. International Economy macros. Application of AI to education.

The problem of integration of artificial intelligence (AI) into any educational system is that it will widen the gap that is already widespread in education. AI tools, including adaptive learning systems, are usually available to a limited number of students and schools, mostly – the wealthy ones.

This discrepancy in number availability promotes a discordance in the quality of education available to differing populations. In third world economies, for instance, a lack of basic infrastructure such as internet and computers further means that the potential of AI technologies in addressing educational gaps is diminished. As a result, this situation leads to an increase in the skill gap and reduced chances for upward income elasticity which in turn strengthens the already existing inequalities. Moreover, the problem is compounded by the need for retraining the teachers, which in poor settings often does not exist (Jain & Jain, 2021; Zhai, 2021) with enough resources.

5.2. Policy and Funding Mechanisms

The policymakers' approach has to change and, in particular, invest in infrastructure and adequately professionally develop the teachers to make any educational opportunities utilizing artificial intelligence technologies to become more accessible.

The development of partnerships between the public and private sector is a good strategy to reduce the costs and also increase the scale of AI uses. The government's funding for AI instruments as well as the provision of encouragements to the private sector can also enhance some of the educational applications of AI tools in the long run.

There are significant ethical issues to deliberate, such as data privacy and reducing bias in algorithms, which should be integrated into policy frameworks that not only address ethical apprehensions but also build conviction among the stakeholders in the education sector (Jain & Jain, 2021; Zhai, 2021). By focusing on these issues, we can promote a fairer and more effective use of AI technologies in education.

5.3. Macroeconomic Impact of an AI-Educated Workforce

The merger of AI and education tools is expected to improve the qualifications and creativity of the workforce, increasing productivity and growth in the economy. Artificial intelligence augmentation of educational systems will tremendously enhance the knowledge and creative skill of the workforce, which will eventually drive up productivity and economic expansion since their new positions are reliant ever more on technological creativity. In more productive economies around the globe, knowledge/skills workers operating in or adjacent to AI will be critical to the transition of future-time sectors.

Alternatively, the economic advantages from the use of AI in education will not be evenly distributed. Countries with established technology infrastructure systems will generally reap a return on the investment in AI-affiliated education quicker and on a larger scale. On the other hand, developing countries earn promising benefits from HP, but this may be disillusioned by the lack of adequate infrastructure and institution.

6. Conclusion and recommendation

Artificial intelligence (AI) integration into the curriculum has the potential to change how people learn and how they teach, both for socioeconomic benefits. But successful application of AI must be wellconsidered and fair in order to bring all actors – particularly those at the bottom – into line with the new technologies. The key to overcome the inequalities between schools that have enough and those that don't requires policies that foster equity, special funding and partnership between public and private sector.

References:

Jain, S., & Jain, Role of Artificial Intelligence in Higher Education - An Empirical Investigation, 2021.

The Position of Artificial Intelligence in the Academic and Administrative Life of Higher Education, Sustainability, 2021.

Zhai, "A Comparison of Artificial Intelligence (AI) in Education 2010–2021," Complexity, 2021.

Zhai, A Survey of Artificial Intelligence (AI) in Education 2010–2020, Complexity, 2021.

3

Generative AI and its Feasibility in the Developing Era: Opportunities, Challenges, and Strategic Pathways for Sustainable Development

Akshay Garg

Generative AI is rapidly gaining recognition as a transformative technological breakthrough with the potential to significantly reshape economies, industries, and societies worldwide. In developing nations, this technology introduces distinct opportunities and challenges that warrant comprehensive investigation. This chapter concentrates on the viability of generative AI within these areas, especially regarding its effects on economic develoment, labor markets, and social equity.

Introduction

With the advancement of generative AI systems, their ability to generate a wide array of content—including text, audio, and video—has the potential to transform the processes by which information is produced and distributed. Nonetheless, the advantages associated with these developments are not evenly available; numerous developing countries encounter considerable obstacles, including insufficient infrastructure and restricted access to state-of-the-art technologies [1]. This gap poses important questions regarding the integration of generative AI in local contexts to enhance inclusive development rather than exacerbating existing inequalities.

By analyzing current literature and identifying gaps in research, this chapter aims to provide a comprehensive understanding of generative AI's role in promoting development. It will investigate how this technology can stimulate economic growth while addressing potential disruptions in labor markets and ensuring social equity. The insights gained will be vital for policymakers and stakeholders seeking to harness generative AI's capabilities responsibly and effectively in the developing era.

The rapid development of generative AI technologies has generated much interest in their use in various industries. For developing economies, these technologies can either be a catalyst for economic development or exacerbate existing inequalities. Policymakers, businesses, and researchers must understand the feasibility of generative AI within these frameworks to leverage its benefits while mitigating risks.

Research Question

What are the feasibility levels of having generative AI technologies used in developing countries, where such technologies can promote economic development and reduce socioeconomic inequality?

Objective of the Research

The core objectives of the research in this paper include:

- Understanding of the current status of the adoption of generative AI in developing countries.
- Identification of the potentials as well as challenges during the implementation.
- Evaluation of the impact of generative AI on economic growth as well as social equity.
- To give actionable proposals to parties involved in the integration of generative AI.

Literature review

This area of study falls under the emerging study at the nexus of technology adoption, economic development, and social equity in developing nations. The literature review gathers all available research to evaluate the prevailing conditions of generative AI implementation, point out associated advantages and obstacles, assess its influence on economic progression and social equity, and offer practical recommendations for various stakeholders.

Current Status of Generative AI Usage

Research findings reveal that although digital transformation is a high-level priority for most emerging countries, the practical usage of emerging technologies such as generative AI is rather limited. Technology adoption studies in small and medium-sized enterprises clearly point out the fact that these firms often concentrate more on the implementation of core information systems rather than adapting advanced forms of technologies like AI[2]. The factors that drive this trend are socio-economic constraints, the lack of proper infrastructure, and inadequate investment in technology. Moreover, research has also implied that community-led initiatives take priority over government-led initiatives with regard to adopting technology, and hence a locality-based approach is essential to enhance the integration of generative AI[2].

Benefits and Barriers to Adoption

Generative AI holds the promise of immense benefit, which primarily revolves around efficiency improvement and innovation. For instance, it may free organizations from mundane tasks, thus making it possible for them to use their resources better on strategic priorities. The main barriers to its adoption are the challenges of ethical dilemmas, issues of data privacy, and the digital divide. A literature review on AI in higher education reveals that while there is enthusiasm for AI's potential to enhance learning experiences, concerns regarding academic integrity and the need for comprehensive training programs persist[3]. These findings underscore the necessity for a balanced approach that maximizes the benefits of generative AI while addressing its associated risks.

Impact on Economic Growth and Social Equity

The effects of generative artificial intelligence on the economic development of developing countries are very great. It can increase the access to information and stimulate new markets and thus encourage entrepreneurship and employment. However, social equity implications are much more complicated. There is a trend that without focused efforts, integration of generative AI will only make existing inequalities worse since only people who already have access to technology will benefit[2][3]. These dynamics are important to consider in the process of understanding how generative AI may foster inclusive economic growth.

Limitations of Literature Reviews

Although current research provides significant insights into the impacts of generative AI on economic growth and inequality in developing countries, there are a number of limitations in the literature that call for further research.

1. Poor Contextual Understanding

Many studies focus on the general potential of generative AI but fail to conduct specific contextual analyses in developing regions of developing countries. There is a high degree of socio-economic, cultural, and political variation in nations and communities in terms of the adoption and implementation of technology. For example, while reports suggest that, in some ways, generative AI might be disruptive even in fields like education and healthcare, localized case studies showing the interrelation between such technologies and currently existing infrastructures and cultural practices are still scarce [5][8]. A more subtle understanding of the contexts is needed for a well-designed strategy that's better suited to particular environments.

2. Lack of Strong Emphasis on Language and Access

Generative AI solutions tend to miss the extremely important problem of language disparities and accessibility in generative AI applications. Most general-purpose generative AI algorithms are designed with dominant language support in mind, disadvantage non-standard languages and dialects common in developing regions [6]. This disparity not only reduces the effectiveness of artificial intelligence technologies but also exacerbates existing inequalities by excluding large portions of the population from benefiting from these innovations. Future research should explore ways in which generative artificial intelligence can be adapted to be inclusive of linguistic diversity, ensuring that its benefits are accessible equally.

3. Ethics and Governance Considerations

Although some articles discuss issues of ethics that are provoked by generative AI, there is a lack of comprehensive frameworks on governance and standards of ethics related to the developing countries [7][9]. Rapid deployment in generative AI technologies results in questions regarding data privacy, misinformation, and accountability; however, there is almost no consensus on how these concerns are managed in various different regulatory contexts. Research should be conducted on establishing context-appropriate ethical guidelines that also take into consideration the more general standards set at international levels.

4. Long-Term Impact Analysis

Most of the existing studies provide a snapshot of the current state of generative AI adoption without longitudinal studies that assess its long-term impacts on economic growth and social equity [4][5]. Therefore, it is important for policymakers to understand how generative AI affects labor markets over time, particularly in terms of job displacement versus job creation. Longitudinal studies may be able to shed light on how generative AI influences industries and employment patterns in developing countries over time.

5. Capacity Building Improvement Strategies

Although some academic articles note the need for competency improvement and capacity building, a gap in specific practical policies especially for developing countries remains open [8]. The next studies should focus on finding the best approaches towards the training programs that empower the individuals with the capabilities required to work effectively with the generative AI technologies. That includes not only technical capabilities but also developing critical thinking and ethical judgment about how AI should be used.

6. Integration into Present Economic Structures

Ultimately, there exists a scarcity of investigation regarding the integration of generative AI within the established economic frameworks of developing nations. Numerous studies frequently emphasize the prospective advantages while neglecting to consider the compatibility of these technologies with traditional industries or informal economies, which are prevalent in many developing areas [7]. It is essential for research to explore methodologies for incorporating generative AI into these pre-existing structures to guarantee that technological progress yields beneficial effects on overall economic stability.

Opportunities for Economic Development in Developing Nations

Generative AI potentially would go a long way toward facilitating economic growth significantly within several areas. Key areas include:

1. Increasing Productivity

The productivity that can be achieved through generative AI enables the automation of many tasks within industries. Such automation in agriculture, manufacturing, and services can lead to a significant reduction in operational costs while allowing for improved output efficiency. For example, supply chains or production techniques can be optimized through tools driven by AI, helping companies scale up operations without a corresponding increase in resources.

2. Innovation

It fosters innovation, most specifically in terms of quick prototyping and product development. This will allow for entrepreneurs in developing countries to use AI and think up new, location specific products and services, thereby spurring economic activity in a place and creating an innovative culture, which will attract more investments and talent.

3. New Markets

The technology can identify unmet needs and create new markets by generating insights from data analysis. For example, generative AI can analyze consumer behavior patterns to inform businesses about emerging trends, allowing them to tailor offerings accordingly. This adaptability can stimulate demand and lead to the establishment of new industries.

4. Education and Skill Development

Generative AI will improve educational content in the form of customized learning experiences. The availability of customized content and assessment will lead to improved education results, thus adequately preparing the workforce for skills in a digital economy. An increasingly skilled workforce will be required to spur the development of the economy while attracting foreign investment.

5. Increased Access to Information

In developing countries, generative AI democratizes access to information since it can generate content in local languages and contexts. Such accessibility empowers the individual and business with knowledge that leads to better decision-making and entrepreneurial activities.

6. Improving Financial Inclusion

AI-based financial technologies can give access to banking services, credit, and insurance products to the underprivileged groups. Generative AI may access data from nontraditional sources to evaluate creditworthiness, which would further allow financial institutions to open their services to those groups that were previously barred from entering the financial system.

This capability can be used in developing countries as a facilitator for sustainable economic growth while addressing existing challenges within their economies.

Challenges in applying generative AI to developing countries

The use of generative AI in developing countries has numerous significant challenges that would affect its application and impact. These are;

1. Infrastructure Limitations

This usually relates to poor Internet connectivity, very few computing capabilities, and no advanced data storage facilities. Such an environment badly challenges the widespread adoption and application of generative AI technologies, as they require very significant computing resources and bandwidth to work properly.

2. Lack of Skills

Often, there is a not sufficient of trained personnel who are conversant in artificial intelligence technologies, such as data scientists, machine learning engineers, and AI engineers. The absence of comprehensive curricula in academic institutions that focus on artificial intelligence and related fields could hinder the creation of a skilled workforce capable of effectively deploying and maintaining generative AI systems. This lack of skills may lead to reliance on outside experts, who may not always be available or affordable.

3. High Implementation Costs

The investment required to prepare for the purchase of generative AI technologies will be too high for most businesses and organizations operating in developing countries. Licensing software and buying hardware and maintaining their operations will discourage potential users, especially SMEs who cannot afford such investments.

4. Data Privacy and Security Concerns

Major hurdles involve privacy and security of data, with the adoption of generative artificial intelligence, especially within areas that have insufficiently enforced or poorly regulated sectors. Fears of data being exploited, accessed without consent, and ethical issues raise barriers for organizations to incorporate AI technologies. In many cases, there is an absence of knowledge about appropriate data protection among stakeholders relevant to the organization.

5. Cultural and Language Differences

The main generative AI systems are often created using the most widely spoken languages and prevalent cultural contexts in place, which can sometimes exclude non-mainstream languages and indigenous customs in developing regions. This limitation may make the applications created not relate to the local communities or address their specific needs.

6. Regulatory Challenges

The absence of clear and defined regulatory structures that govern the use of artificial intelligence technologies can create vagueness for organizations wanting to utilize generative AI. Where there are unclear principles governing ethical use, responsibility, and compliance, organizations will be hesitant to adopt the technologies due to fears related to potential litigation or reputational damage.

7. Resistance to Change

Cultural views on the adoption of technology can be a significant challenge. In some cases, resistance may come from established industries or communities that are skeptical about the benefits of generative AI or fear job loss due to automation. Overcoming this resistance requires effective change management and active community engagement.

8. Limited Access to Quality Data

The effectiveness of generative AI models depends much on good quality data for training. Availability of large datasets is limited in many developing countries, often due to poor data collection methods or inadequate digitization in many sectors. This would, therefore, limit the applications of generative AI.

9. Ethical Considerations

This would be raising ethical issues concerned with bias, fairness, and accountability in deploying this kind of AI. The reason is that unchecked deployment could easily end up promoting social inequality or other unwanted consequences for vulnerable populations.

Major challenges in accessing generative AI technologies in developing countries:

Several key challenges in using generative artificial intelligence technologies plague individuals and organizations alike within developing countries. These fall under the broad categories of infrastructural, economic, educational, regulatory, and socio-cultural factors:

1. Infrastructure Barrier

- Internet Connectivity Barriers: Most developing countries experience erratic or slow internet connectivity. This is one of the most fundamental prerequisites to connect with cloud-based AI and applications. This deficiency in connectivity is a barrier to proper utilization of generative AI technologies.
- Inadequate computational resources: Generative AI mostly requires a high amount of computational power, which is rarely found in developing regions. This issue is compounded by the high costs that come with expensive hardware and software.

2. Economic Barriers

- Cost of Technology: The upfront cost that is involved with the generative AI technologies, including software licenses, hardware purchase, and maintenance costs is way beyond the reach of the businesses and organizations in the developing countries, especially SMEs.
- Limited Access to Financial Capital: Most start-ups and companies in developing regions lack access to sufficient funding to implement technology; this is mainly because of a lack of venture capital or investment options focused on innovative technologies such as artificial intelligence.

3. Challenges in Learning

There can often be skill shortages in the availability of those trained individuals with education regarding artificial intelligence and machine learning. Educational institutions may sometimes have no programs that focus specifically on these areas, thus the limitations of developing a workforce competent enough to implement and run such generative AI technologies.

- Lack of awareness: A sizeable percentage of potential users will not be aware of the benefits or applications of generative AI, and hence, underutilization and unwillingness to adopt will be inevitable.

4. Regulatory Barriers

Weak Regulatory Frameworks Weak regulatory frameworks concerning the adoption and usage of AI technologies leave organizations in ambiguity while making decisions on its use. The absence of strong regulations concerning data privacy issues, ethical usage, or accountability prevents businesses from investing heavily in generative AI

- Intellectual Property Concerns : Intellectual property rights issues concerning AI generated products may not draw businesses towards working with generative AI technologies.

5. Socio-Cultural Barriers

- Cultural Resistance: Locals and traditional industries would resist new technologies because they fear the loss of jobs and a threat to the status quo.
- Language and Cultural Context: Generative AI models are often created with the aim of supporting dominant languages and dominant cultural paradigms. This limits the effectiveness of AI in various communities and populations.

6. Data Accessibility Challenges

- Lack of Proper Data Access: Generative AI requires large amounts of quality data to train the systems. In many developing countries, the lack of proper data collection or poor digitization in various fields limits the availability of large data sets.

7. Ethical Concerns

- Issues Pertaining to Bias and Fairness: Apprehensions regarding bias within artificial intelligence algorithms may deter organizations from embracing generative AI technologies. Should stakeholders believe that these technologies could perpetuate preexisting inequalities or result in inequitable outcomes, they might exhibit hesitance in their engagement with such innovations.

Assessing Matrix of Economic growth and social equity

The quantitative as well as qualitative techniques will need to be holistically merged in order to gauge the effects of generative AI on economic growth and social equity. Some of the strategies, based on the insight drawn from the literature are discussed as follows:

1. Formation of Evaluation Frameworks

A clear framework is needed for the assessment of social impacts of generative AI systems. The framework should group different impacts into measurable areas, such as:

- Economic Indicators: Measuring productivity, job creation, and revenue growth in industries adopting generative AI.
- Social Equity Indicators: Measuring technology access among different populations, including income groups, education levels, and regional disparities.[10]

2. Quantitative Analysis

Economic indicators will be gathered in advance and after the adoption of generative AI technologies using quantitative methods. This could include:

- Surveys and Collection of Economic Data: A survey will be conducted from business firms and communities to collect data relating to the shift in levels of productivity, employment, and changes in income levels.
- Statistical Analysis: This will be through the use of econometric models to understand the generative AI adoption relationship with various measures of economic growth. This can involve regression analysis to establish correlations and causal relationships.

3. Qualitative Research

The integration of qualitative insights with quantitative data will give a better understanding of the consequences that come with generative AI.

- Interviews and Focus Groups: Interviewing different stakeholders such as business leaders, policy makers, and community members to get individual stories and opinions about how generative AI influences their respective fields.
- Case Studies: A more comprehensive case study of a particular industry or community embracing generative AI can reveal both positive and negative consequences of the process.

4. Social Equity Assessment

To clearly observe the impacts on social equity:

- Access Analysis: Understand who has access to these technologies and identify barriers which hinder access to marginalized populations. This may include statistical demographic studies in terms of gender, income level, and education.
- Impact Assessments: Assess which industries experience more job losses and job gains due to the influence of generative AI. This would necessarily mean examining changes in dynamics of labor markets and needed reskilling for involved workers.

5. Long-term Impact Tracking

The long-term impact of generative AI needs to be measured over time through longitudinal studies. This includes:

- Monitoring Economic Indicators: These are changes in performance measures of the economy that will happen over several years since the technology implementation of generative AI.
- Ongoing Community Engagement: Engaging with communities regularly to track how equity and access are perceived at later times as technologies change.

6. Policy Recommendations

Policy recommendations based on conclusions from evaluations:

- Formulation of guidelines: This entails developing policy recommendations that ensure equal access to generative artificial intelligence technologies. However, these should address the ethical concerns of bias and privacy.

- Commitment to education and training: Resources are allocated toward educational frameworks preparing the workforce for a technology-based economy, thereby ensuring all demographic groups can benefit from technological advancements.

Actionable recommendations to stakeholders

This end has to be supported by the following actionable recommendations on all stakeholders: governments, businesses, educational institutions, and civil society.

1. Investment in Infrastructure Development

- Improve Digital Connectivity: The government should prioritize investment in internet infrastructure to guarantee reliable, high-speed connectivity, particularly in rural and underserved regions. Collaborations between the public and private sectors can play a key role in expanding access.
- Improving Computing Resources. Engage programs that make computing resources available and affordable for use, such as cloud services and hardware designed for AI.

2. Education and Training

- Curriculum Integration: All levels of education, starting from elementary school up to college, should expose students to AI and data science. This also includes dedicated programs for generative AI.
- Training Programs: Provide dedicated training programs to the existing workforce to get equipped in AI technologies. Tech companies might be able to collaborate in the designing of such programs so that they meet the requirements of the industry.

3. Enhance Awareness and Comprehension

- Awareness Initiatives: Implement initiatives designed to inform businesses and communities regarding the advantages and uses of generative AI. Such efforts can clarify the complexities of the technology and promote its adoption.

- Workshops and Conferences: Coordinate workshops and conferences that assemble stakeholders from diverse sectors to exchange knowledge and exemplary practices concerning the implementation of generative AI.

4. Implement Regulatory Frameworks

- Set Clear Guidelines: Governments need to set clear regulatory frameworks which should include data privacy, ethical use of AI, and accountability. Such guidelines will help instill trust among the users and promote responsible usage.
- Promote Ethical AI Usage: Provide organizations with resources and frameworks for bias, transparency, and fairness in AI systems.

5. Facilitate Access to Funding

- Develop Funding Programs: Introduce grants, subsidies, or low-interest loans specifically dedicated to the support of businesses in adopting generative AI technologies. These programs may reduce some of the initial costs that hinder business entry.
- Encourage Venture Capital Involvement: Facilitate investments in start-ups focused on generative AI by creating conducive environments for venture capitalists through tax incentives or investment matching schemes.

6. Intersectoral Cooperation

- Public-Private Partnerships: Facilitate collaborative efforts among governmental bodies, private enterprises, and non-profit organizations to pool resources, share knowledge, and leverage expertise in the implementation of generative artificial intelligence.
- Community Engagement: Engage local communities in the creation and implementation of generative artificial intelligence solutions to guarantee that these technologies meet their particular requirements and challenges.

7. Track Impact and Refine Strategies

- Mechanism for Evaluation: Put mechanisms in place to track the impact of generative AI on economic growth and social equity over time. It includes tracking data on the number of jobs created, changes in productivity, and disparities in access.

- Adaptation of Policies Based on Feedback: Use feedback from evaluation to adapt policies and strategies regarding the adoption of generative AI, keeping them relevant and effective over time.

8. Support Research and Innovation

- Support Local Research Initiatives: Support research projects for developing applications of generative AI in local contexts to solve problems in a specific region.
- Promote Innovation Hubs: Develop innovation hubs or incubators that support the development of startups in generative AI solutions for developing countries.

Performance Measurement for Stakeholders

There is a need to use a set of performance metrics that cover economic, operational, social, and user satisfaction to measure the effectiveness of implementing generative AI. Some of the critical performance metrics include:

1. Economic Performance Metrics

- Revenue Growth: Measure the amount of revenue generated from companies that have implemented the use of generative AI technologies compared to the previous years.
- Cost Savings: Determine the reductions in costs of operations as a direct result of deploying generative AI, including reduced labor costs or improved resource allocation.
- ROI: Find the ROI of generative AI projects by determining and comparing the financial benefits secured with the investment made within the deployment stage.

2. Operational Efficiency Metrics

- Productivity Improvements: Measure productivity level changes, such as output per employee or time taken to complete tasks before and after adopting generative AI solutions.
- Process Automation Rate: Percentage of processes automated through generative AI, which would represent the degree of operational transformation.

- Time to Market: Study the decreases in the time cycle for product or service design and launch due to the capacities of generative AI.

3. Social Impact Metrics

- Job Creation vs. Job Displacement: The number of newly created jobs in sectors related to generative AI as compared to the number of jobs lost due to automation, thereby ascertaining the net employment effect.
- Access and Equity Metrics: Track if generative AI technologies are opening up more access to services and opportunities by income, education, location, and so on.
- Community Engagement: Monitor the participation and feedback from the community on generative AI adoption, monitoring fairness and equity perceptions.

4. User Satisfaction Metrics

- User Adoption Rates: Track the rate at which employees or end-users within an organization are adopting generative AI products, focusing on aspects like adoption speed and overall usability.
- User Satisfaction Surveys: Conduct surveys to gather feedback from users regarding their experiences with generative AI products, with a focus on usability, effectiveness, and overall satisfaction.
- Training Effectiveness: Assess the impact of training programs on the acceptance of generative AI by evaluating user confidence and proficiency levels both before and after training.

5. Quality and Performance Metrics

- Output Quality: Measure the output quality delivered by AI systems in accuracy, relevance, and content or products' creativity.
- Error Rates: Track error rates on the generative AI system in producing its outputs, which measures their reliability to identify areas to improve further.

6. Innovation Metrics

- New Products/Services Launched: Track the number of new products or services developed with generative AI tools during a period.

- Patent Filings: Track patent filings for inventions based on the output of generative AI applications as an indicator of technological advancements.

7. Compliance and Ethical Metrics

- Data Privacy Compliance Rate: Track compliance with data privacy regulations and ethics in the use of generative AI technologies.
- Bias evaluation scores: Assess bias in AI-created outputs through periodic audits, ensuring that decision-making processes remain fair and equitable.

8. Longitudinal Studies

- Perform longitudinal studies to monitor the developments over time in terms of economic performance, social impacts, and user satisfaction measurement. This helps understand effects that last over time from implementing generative AI.

The better integration of generative AI technologies can be facilitated with established best practices and actionable metrics for stakeholders, thus allowing for optimal potential benefits in terms of both economic development and social equity.

Future Research Directions

Although this research offers an in-depth analysis of generative AI adoption in developing countries, it has a number of limitations that should be taken into account. First and foremost, the research mainly highlights a narrow selection of developing countries, which might not capture the diverse socio-economic conditions and technological environments prevalent in all the developing regions. Consequently, the findings derived may not be universally applicable, and there is a potential for unique issues and opportunities related to particular countries or areas to be overlooked. Additionally, depending on existing literature and secondary sources of information can introduce biases or leave gaps, particularly in areas with limited empirical research. One of the key challenges posed by the fast-evolving nature of generative AI technology is that the pace of innovation is so rapid that research findings can become outdated quickly, requiring constant updates to stay relevant. The study also heavily relies on qualitative and quantitative methods, which may not fully capture the diverse range of experiences and perspectives from all stakeholders. Although interviews and surveys can offer some valuable insights, they are unlikely to fully represent the complexity of reality as experienced by all parties involved in the adoption of generative AI. This limits the need for richer case studies that explore specific examples of generative AI use in various industries to help better understand its impacts on local communities.

In thinking about future directions, future researchers have considerable opportunities to build on this study by addressing the limitations identified above and expanding the scope of investigation. One promising direction for future research is conducting longitudinal studies aimed at capturing the long-term effects of integrating generative AI into economic development and social welfare. Such questions may lead to crucial insights into how generative AI impacts labor markets, productivity levels, and access to resources in developing countries.

Research should also be conducted on cultural factors that affect the uptake and perception of generative artificial intelligence technologies. By understanding how regional traditions, principles, and convictions can influence the adoption of technology, interventions can be developed which fit into community values and enhance equal access to the benefits of generative AI. Comparative studies conducted across different developing countries would thus bring crucial findings on best practices and strategies for successful implementation.

Another area that needs to be explored is the ethical implications of deploying generative artificial intelligence in developing countries. Future researchers can delve into how biases embedded in AI algorithms affect the marginalized communities and propose frameworks that will help ensure fairness and accountability in AI deployment. This includes data governance approaches to ensure that data collection and use are done in ways that respect ethical standards while protecting individual rights to privacy.

With further advancement of generative artificial intelligence technologies, the need will be ongoing to explore and understand new applications and impacts across the sectors of health care, education, agriculture, and finance. One of the important research components will be the ways in which generative AI can confront specific challenges from these sectors specifically in developing countries in order to maximize its beneficial impact.

It is with these metrics that stakeholders get an in-depth understanding of the consequences that come along with implementing generative AI within their respective organizations and communities. Continued monitoring and assessment will enable stakeholders to make informed decisions, adapt their strategies, and maximize the benefits associated with this transformative technology.

In a nutshell, the opportunities for implementing generative artificial intelligence in developing countries are vast, while challenges are enormous. The current study underscores the revolutionary capacity of generative AI for economic development, effectiveness, and innovation in a vast array of domains, but also calls attention to crucial barriers to effective implementation, such as infrastructural deficiencies, skills gaps, and ethical considerations.

To fully benefit from the generative AI and ensure social equity, the approach of stakeholders must be multi-faceted by investing in infrastructure, education, and training, besides having clear regulatory frameworks in place. Diverse stakeholders can be brought together and collaboration across sectors can be fostered to ensure an environment that is amenable to responsible AI adoption.

Moreover, periodic review of the effects of generative AI on economic performance and social outcomes should be ensured to help this technology's implementation assist in meeting developmental goals. With these advances in technology, policymakers, firms, and societies need to adapt and innovate to solve new problems that arise. Conclusion Generative AI has the ability to be a strong instrument of inclusive growth and sustainable development in developing countries if adopted with appropriate policies.

In conclusion, as much as this study may provide rich insights into implementing generative AI in developing countries, it simultaneously accentuates enormous limitations that would be ripe for subsequent investigators to look into. Such areas might include longitudinal investigation, the cultural context within which people operate ethical sensitivities, and applications specific to multiple sectors or industries. Future investigation into all these areas could further knowledge regarding how generative AI responsibly and effectively can be used towards furthering sustainable development as well as social equity through diverse settings.

Citations

[1] Artificial Intelligence In Developing Countries: The Impact Of Generative Artificial Intelligence (AI) Technologies For Development Information Development 14 September 2023 from https://www.semanticscholar.org/paper/5a5e03c3c8bf5052a99f4631e874b1e608e59319

[2] Navigating Digital Transformation And Technology Adoption: A Literature Review From Small And Medium-Sized Enterprises In Developing Countries Sustainability 12 July 2024 from https://www.semanticscholar.org/paper/244d63b26bfdd59b9c15617f0593911706470507

[3] A Systematic Literature Review Of Attitudes, Intentions And Behaviours Of Teaching Academics Pertaining To AI And Generative AI (Genai) In Higher Education: An Analysis Of Genai Adoption Using The UTAUT Framework Australasian Journal of Educational Technology 16 December 2024 from https://www.semanticscholar.org/paper/8aa035778b17e14d209f37c9837c7c84ee61201c

[4] Transforming Teacher Education In Developing Countries: The Role Of Generative AI In Bridging Theory And Practice Submitted on 16 Nov 2024 (v1), last revised 21 Nov 2024 (this version, v3) from https://arxiv.org/abs/2411.10718

[5] The Influence And Impact Of Livelihood Capitals On Livelihood Diversification Strategies In Developing Countries: A Systematic Literature Review Environ Sci Pollut Res Int. 2023 May 17;30(27):69882–69898 from https://pmc.ncbi.nlm.nih.gov/articles/PMC10239380/

[6] How Language Gaps Constrain Generative AI Development International Journal of Comparative Studies in International Relations and Development , 11 November 2023 from https://www.semanticscholar.org/paper/8de74be04669b0b98bb997b93bc25678b3432729

[7] Effective Generative AI Implementation In Developing Country Universities Conference on Algebraic Informatics, 25 June 2024 from https://www.semanticscholar.org/paper/9ae9ce137dfc576ab7127a75d84d4657d413b58d

[8] Artificial Intelligence In Developing Countries: Bridging The Gap Between Potential And Implementation Computer Science & IT Research Journal, 3 December 2023 from https://www.semanticscholar.org/paper/3d7d961a9278d53f004238e83715d66be6fb1b23

[9] Deepfakes, Misinformation, And Disinformation In The Era Of Frontier AI, Generative AI, And Large AI Models Submitted on 29 Nov 2023 from https://arxiv.org/abs/2311.17394

[10] Evaluating The Social Impact Of Generative AI Systems In Systems And Society Submitted on 9 Jun 2023 (v1), last revised 28 Jun 2024 (this version, v4) from https://arxiv.org/abs/2306.05949

4

Revolutionizing Psychology Training with the Help of Artificial Intelligence

Neha Kaushik
Empowering Psychology Teachers and Students
Research Associate, IILM University, Gurugram
Email: neha.kaushik.phd22@iilm.edu

The human mind is the most complex entity in the world, and understanding it is the most crucial task. As per the definition of psychology by the American Psychological Association, "psychology is a study of mind and behavior," which consists of how people think, behave, feel, etc. The scope of this field is wider than the social sciences. Many other disciplines can be easily blended with psychology, such as business, marketing, sociology, philosophy, technology, etc. The field has influenced many different fields over the past few years. Similarly, over the past two to three years, artificial intelligence has also influenced the world. A few years ago, no one would have thought of a technology that would be so close to human intelligence. Its humane responses have impressed many to the extent that people from diverse backgrounds, all groups, and every kind of industry have started to use it already to improve the efficiency of their work. You can ask artificial intelligence (AI) to write a letter to your friend, and it will write it in such a way that it will create the impression that you wrote it. From writing a letter to using it for research work to drafting an email, all can be done with the help of artificial intelligence. This sounds impressive. Right? Indeed, it is. However, one needs to keep the ethical practice in mind while using it. You must be wondering that if artificial intelligence has served professionals in all areas, then there must be some advantages to the professionals in the field of education too, right? The answer is yes. Educators have also started to use it. However, a lot of people are still not aware of its efficient use. It has been observed that their usage is restricted to drafting mail or sending messages. In the current chapter, we will be discussing how teachers and students can use artificial intelligence to make their learning process easy and effective. In the digital world, where we are bombarded with information, it becomes difficult for people to pay attention to relevant information (Subramanian, 2017), especially in the classroom setup where student engagement is crucial for making the lecture successful. With the help of artificial intelligence, we can make lectures so engaging and captivating for students, especially in subjects like psychology, which have practical and theoretical-based papers. Such subjects are difficult for students to understand in a normal classroom setup.

Integration of Artificial Intelligence in Psychology

Artificial intelligence can be described as the ability of machines to complete tasks that usually require human intelligence. These tasks can be anything related to cognition, such as decision-making, problem-solving, speech and face recognition, etc. (Triansyahet al., 2023). Artificial intelligence is not just limited to the technology fields, but it is essential to remember its integration with other fields like cognitive sciences. Its integration with other fields such as linguistics, neurobiology, philosophy, etc. makes it an interdisciplinary study (Pfeifer, 1988). In recent times, artificial developments have shown many limitations in human rationality while showing that computers can be highly creative. This opens a new way of studying human creativity, which comes under the field of psychology, opening new avenues of novel experiments and the development of new theories of creativity in cognition (Gobet and Sala, 2019). In addition to this, cognition in artificial intelligence is not just limited to the creativity part, but other significant parts of psychology, like emotions, are also involved. It can contribute to the study of emotions as it shows a common language for representing information about ideas, plans, and tricky structures that can provide valuable metaphors for understanding human emotions (Pfeifer, 1988). Artificial intelligence provides exciting opportunities for psychology educators and learners to participate in and contribute to the development of artificial intelligence. However, students should be trained well to avoid the overuse of artificial intelligence. Artificial intelligence literacy, including its effective usage, such as personalized learning source recommendations, and its negative impact of overusing it, should be elaborately discussed with the students to avoid overdependence. This should be done to ensure the right practice of using artificial intelligence.

Use of Artificial Intelligence for Psychology Teachers

1. Seamless Psychology Lesson Design

A plethora of information on the internet has led to a situation where there is cognitive overload. And as the saying goes, excess of anything is not good. The same things happen to us as well. This cognitive overload has led to a situation where it has started to impact cognitive abilities (including attention span), especially students (Haroutunian-Gordon, 2019). Over the years, there has been a decrease in attention span. The trend of watching long movies has shifted to scrolling reels because attention spans have reduced a lot. So, making students learn something in a classroom with such short attention spans is a real challenge for teachers. Since psychology lectures differ from other disciplines, the lecture delivery approaches also become very distinct from other disciplines. It involves detailed examples, case studies, lots of reflective activities, reflective discussions, demo sessions, role plays, movie analysis, mindfulness-based activities, therapeutic techniques, etc. Tools like Yippty, Classpoint AI can be used to generate questions for class. For instance, planning a session on cognitive biases sometimes gets difficult and confusing for students to understand. With the help of artificial intelligence (AI), the sessions can be planned in such a way that students find it relatable and simple to understand, depending on who we are teaching based on the age group, background, etc. AI can provide customization options, as everything is just a few clicks away for people. It can also foster an environment of self-learning (Lin, 2024). In this way, students can grasp the concept faster than usual. Similarly, students can easily understand subjects like biopsychology and cognitive psychology with the help of artificial intelligence tools available. In fact, the help of motion tracking and analysis of students' behavior, class engagement, and emotional states, can help the psychology teacher adjust the pace of the class accordingly (Raihan et al., 2024).

2. Customized Assessments and Feedback

Every student is different, and every student comes with different abilities and ways to learn things. Then, why do we restrict ourselves to all the students if their ability to learn is different? Artificial intelligence can help in forming question papers in such a way that teachers can make a question paper based on the student's ability (Mujtaba and Mahapatra, 2020). Artificial intelligence can form a customized assessment based on the students' intellect, academic background, and other factors. For instance, students who struggle with writing long answers can be assessed based on the short answer type of questions in the examination. And making the customized assessment won't be a time-consuming process with the help of artificial intelligence. In addition to this, artificial intelligence analyzes the student's responses and can share timely personalized feedback on their responses, which can help students to work on their weak areas by implementing required changes in their study patterns (Vetrivel et al., 2024).

3. Thought-provoking Discussions

Class engagement has always been an important factor that defines the quality of the session. Access to chatbots has proven to be a useful tool so far and can be used to enhance class engagement. We can easily ask as many questions as we want with the accessibility of the 27*4 availability option. Psychology educators can utilize chatbots to make mind-stimulating questions for class. Tools like ChatGPT can help in finding stimulating questions for class discussions, leading to healthy, mind-stimulating conversations (Lin, 2024). These discussions can be application-based questions. These questions can foster an environment of healthy, engaging discussion in a classroom, which can help students understand the concept as well as the perspectives of their classmates. This can also work as a team-building activity for students.

4. Assistance in Research Work

Research has always been a crucial part of academia, and psychology is a field where it plays an important role. Over the years, the idea of publishing or perishing has increased the pressure to publish so much that it has started to impact the academic profile of many educators. Managing it with class content preparation and other administrative work makes it difficult for professionals to get into the zone of doing an in-depth study. It can streamline the research process. Artificial intelligence can assist us in finding the current research trends in psychology. Furthermore, it can save enough time for researchers if used efficiently, which they can utilize to enhance the quality of their research papers by focusing on adding graphs, charts, tables, detailed analysis, and a better presentation of the paper. The time that they used to spend on finding existing research, which is now simple to gather, can improve the writing style and reduce grammatical errors too (Polonevych, 2024). Tools like Sci-Space, Litmaps, Research Rabbit, Consensus and other tools can help in literature review; Grammarly, Quillbot and Paperpal and other tools can be used for academic writing purposes. However, researchers cannot rely on artificial intelligence. The researcher must avoid using artificial intelligence to write papers on their behalf; research papers have to be written by the researcher only, since it is not ethical, and most plagiarism detection software has the option of AI detection on their website. They can easily detect whether the content is AI-generated. Furthermore, some artificial intelligence tools have the option to chat with the paper, where researchers can ask artificial intelligence to share the summary of the paper or the methodology, and it shows you the same. You can extract anything from the research paper as per your requirements. Despite its easy accessibility, it is crucial to keep ethical considerations in mind, especially when taking AI assistance in research work. Any kind of malpractice should be avoided; teachers must convey this point to their students too (Cost et al., 2024).

5. Simplified Administrative Work

The teaching part of the academic career is one responsibility. However, the job profile of an academic consists of many other responsibilities. One such task consists of the administrative work that an academician is supposed to fulfill. From taking attendance to updating everything on time to ensure the smooth flow of work. Most administrative work can be eased with the help of artificial intelligence if one knows how to use it effectively. Utilizing artificial intelligence for administrative tasks like updating grades and other things can be of beneficial use by using the time for mentoring and guiding students (Ahmad et al., 2022). Also, time saved from artificial intelligence for administrative work can be utilized to enhance the research quality, which can ultimately lead to a good-quality publication and a strong research profile.

6. Utilization of Virtual Reality in Psychology

Technology advancement has reached a level where one can get the real experience virtually. Virtual reality has always been an intriguing topic for many. Visual learning content easily catches students' attention and enables a more engaging class environment, which is important for learning (Ahmad and Halim, 2024). When the classroom environment is different from the typical lecture session, students tend to engage better and feel motivated to learn something (Gogiashvili and Demetrashvili, 2024). The experience it provides has shaken the world. Integrating virtual reality with artificial intelligence can significantly improve the classroom setup for psychology students, especially in psychology classes where practical experience plays an important role. Virtual reality with the integration of artificial intelligence is enough to stimulate the environment for learning therapies in a classroom. Scenarios created by virtual reality give a real-life experience where students can easily practice assessments, psychological experiments, therapies, and other psychological skills required for them to become effective therapists in the future (Pazukhina, 2024). For instance, psychology students can learn to apply relaxation techniques well if there is any stressful situation created with the help of virtual reality. It can be effective in the case of mindfulness therapies if used correctly. There is research evidence indicating the use of virtual reality in cases of anxiety issues. A virtual demonstration can be an effective way to teach therapeutic techniques to psychology students. Furthermore, virtual reality can simplify complex psychological topics for students. However, ethical considerations need to be considered before using it (Costa et al., 2024).

Use of Artificial Intelligence for Psychology Students

1. 24*7 Expert Guidance

Teachers answer all the queries that students bring into the classroom. However, sometimes it is not possible to answer all the questions in the classroom. Also, not every student in the classroom is confident enough to ask a question in a room full of students. Sometimes students tend to go back and study to find the answer. Sometimes they proceed, and sometimes they struggle to find their answers. In such scenarios, artificial intelligence can be helpful for students. AI chatbots answer queries in a span of a few seconds. Furthermore, the customization option provided by artificial intelligence benefits students a lot. Students can access study material any time they want and can get the responses based on their difficulty level, which can also enhance their engagement and comprehension in the learning process (Susilo, 2024). For instance, if one finds it easy to read something in an easy language, then artificial intelligence can simplify the complex topic for them.

2. Learning of Psychological Concepts through Visual Learning

People learn things better when they see them rather than when they read them. Some psychological concepts are difficult and take time to understand when one reads them since it is a practical-based paper. In such cases, a visual representation of the concept can help students grasp it well. It has been observed that visual presentation makes it easier to understand complex concepts. (Bobek and Tversky, 2016). For example, students are often scared of brain parts and their functions; however, visual representation with the help of artificial intelligence can make it look vibrant and interesting enough for learners to study.

3. Cognitive Training Games for Practice

To improve the cognitive functioning of the brain, one should practice cognitive games to enhance cognitive functions, which are important in our day-to-day lives, like problem-solving skills, decision-making, attention span, memory, etc., with the help of artificial intelligence. Psychology students can explore such activities with the help of artificial intelligence to enhance their skills. Additionally, these games can be used in their therapy practice later on with clients with various cognitive difficulties. These cognitive games can be adapted according to the pace of learning of the students, which can help them eliminate the challenges to enhance their cognitive functions (Granda et al., 2024).

4. Experience of Real World Scenarios in the Virtual World

Before starting a career as a professional in the field of psychology, a therapist needs loads of training and practice. However, it has been observed that due to a lack of adequate training, students face various challenges when they deal with real clients at the beginning of their careers. In such cases, proper practice of therapy techniques in sessions becomes highly important. Artificial intelligence can provide students with experience of real-world scenarios in a demo session where students can get hands-on learning experience. Chatbots can be used for role-playing sessions when the chances of impacting the other person are very low, yet chances of applying the therapeutic techniques in real life can be higher, with the option of immediate feedback (Lin, 2024; Kanwan et al., 2024).

5. Mental Health Tracking

In recent years, many artificial intelligence tools have emerged, enabling easy monitoring of mental health regularly. It can track mental health. It can monitor everything, from mood to anxiety levels. This can help in planning further steps. Chatbots can provide some mental health tips that one can follow to improve their mental health. It can reduce the stigma and encourage help-seeking behavior (Kapoor and Goel, 2022). For example, in the case of mild stress levels, it might suggest something that makes you feel more relaxed. Not only can you do it to yourself, but this way, the possibility of helping a mass audience all at once becomes an effortless option. Although this cannot necessarily provide a specific solution to your problem, in cases of moderate to severe issues, one needs to reach out to mental health professionals without delay.

6. Practice Made Easy Now

Students often feel stressed about the exams, and they don't feel very confident about their preparation. To reduce exam stress, students can practice for their assessment using the help of artificial intelligence. They can practice model tests, papers, and application-based questions to assess their level of understanding, which can help them identify their weak areas and provide immediate feedback that can help students adjust their learning styles and pace for a better understanding of the concept for their examination (Sumanth et al., 2024).

Precautions for Using Artificial Intelligence in Psychology

A report states that about 62% of educators use artificial intelligence either sometimes or always, which shows that artificial intelligence started to be a part of teaching aids in the educational system (Learning, 2024). They use it for activities like planning brainstorming activities or developing a session plan for students. However, it was reported that educators feel uncomfortable with the idea of students using artificial intelligence. There are certain precautions that one needs to keep in mind while using it. To ensure ethical practice, educators should get the proper training in artificial intelligence usage because improper training and lack of awareness about ethical practices can lead to malpractices, which must be avoided (Zuhu, 2024). Also, educators can spread awareness and train students about the right usage of artificial intelligence along with its limitations. Some artificial intelligence tools should be verified in terms of privacy, consent, and ethical use of data. Students should be informed about the relevant and safe tools for improving their academic performance. Also, overusing artificial intelligence should be avoided. It should be considered an addition to improve the quality of psychology classes conducted by experienced human educators to foster critical thinking and creativity, which is the main goal of education. It should not impact the existing practices and job roles (Zaman, 2024; Sagin et al., 2023).

Conclusion

There are many benefits of artificial intelligence in psychology. And the above-mentioned are a few of them. Artificial intelligence can improve the quality of work and save a lot of time if used effectively and efficiently. However, ethical consideration needs to be given. Precautions should be considered while using it. Also, it cannot substitute for the student-teacher relationship, which is essential for student learning. It should be considered an addition in the classroom; it cannot affect any existing role in a psychology classroom.

References

Ahmad, S. F., Alam, M. M., Rahmat, M. K., Mubarik, M. S., &Hyder, S. I. (2022). Academic and administrative role of artificial intelligence in education. Sustainability, 14(3), 1101. https://doi.org/10.3390/su14031101

Ahmad, M., &AbdHalim, N. D. (2024). Audio-Visual Learning in Secondary School: A Review of Advantages and Challenges in Education. Innovative Teaching and Learning Journal, 8(1), 15-23. https://doi.org/10.11113/itlj.v8.153

Bobek, E., &Tversky, B. (2016). Creating visual explanations improves learning. Cognitive research: principles and implications, 1, 1-14. https://doi.org/10.1186/s41235-016-0031-6

Carnegie Learning. (2024). Thestate of AI in education: Artificial intelligence in education 2024 report. https://discover.carnegielearning.com/hubfs/PDFs/2024-AI-in-Ed-Report.pdf

Costa, C., Husain-Habib, N., & Reiter, A. (2024). Integrating AI Into Education: Successful Strategies, Ideas, and Tools From Psychology Instructors. Teaching of Psychology, (0). https://doi.org/10.1177/00986283241297

Gobet, F., &Sala, G. (2019). How Artificial Intelligence Can Help Us Understand Human Creativity. Frontiers in Psychology, 10. https://doi.org/10.3389/fpsyg.2019.01401

Gogiashvili, S., &Demetrashvili, A. (2022). The Impact of Online Learning on Visual Learners in the HEIs for Sustainable Development and Well-Being. The Journal Of Development Studies, 3(3). https://doi.org/10.52340/jds.2022.03.03.02

Granda, B. S., Inzhivotkina, Y., Apolo, M. F. I., &Fajardo, J. G. U. (2024). Educational innovation: Exploring the Potential of Generative Artificial Intelligence in cognitive schema building. Edutec, RevistaElectrónica de TecnologíaEducativa, (89), 44-63. (translated) https://doi.org/10.21556/edutec.2024.89.3251

Haroutunian-Gordon, S. (2009). Learning to teach through discussion: The art of turning the soul. Yale University Press.

Kapoor, A., &Goel, S. (2022, April). Applications of Conversational AI in Mental Health: A Survey. In 2022 6th International Conference on Trends in Electronics and Informatics (ICOEI) (pp. 1013-1016). IEEE. https://doi.org/10.1109/ICOEI53556.2022.9777127

Kaswan, K. S., Dhatterwal, J. S., &Ojha, R. P. (2024). AI in personalized learning. In Advances in Technological Innovations in Higher Education (pp. 103-117). CRC Press.

Lin, Y. (2024). New psychological education: Leveraging the power of ChatGPT and artificial intelligence .Applied and Computational Engineering, 36, 220-224. http://doi.org/10.54254/2755-2721/36/20230450

Mujtaba, D. F., &Mahapatra, N. R. (2020, December). Artificial intelligence in computerized adaptive testing. In 2020 International Conference on Computational Science and Computational Intelligence (CSCI) (pp. 649-654). IEEE. http://doi.org/10.1109/CSCI51800.2020.00116

Pazukhina, Svetlana. (2024). Possibilities Of Using VR Technologies In The Process Of Teaching Psychology To Students In Psychological And Pedagogical Classes. Child in a Digital World. 1. 32-33. 10.61365/forum.2024.014.

Pfeifer, R. (1988). Artificial Intelligence Models of Emotion (Vol. 44, pp. 287–320). springernetherlands. https://doi.org/10.1007/978-94-009-2792-6_12

Polonevych, O.. (2024). Use of artificial intelligence in the organization of scientific research. Connectivity. 169. http://doi.org/10.31673/2412-9070.2024.030306.

Raihan, M., Debnath, A., Adhikary, P., Masud, M., Meshref, H., &Bairagi, A. K. (2024). Bridging Technology and Psychology: AI-Driven Analysis of Student's Class Lecture Activity for Improved Learning Outcomes. IEEE Access. https://doi.org/10.1109/ACCESS.2024.3474848

Sağın, F. G., Özkaya, A. B., Tengiz, F., Geyik, Ö. G., &Geyik, C. (2024). Current evaluation and recommendations for the use of artificial intelligence tools in education. Turkish Journal of Biochemistry, 48(6), 620-625. https://doi.org/10.1515/tjb-2023-0254

Sumanth, N. S., Priya, S. V., Sankari, M., &Kamatchi, K. S. (2024, April). AI-Enhanced Learning Assistant Platform. In 2024 International Conference on Inventive Computation Technologies (ICICT) (pp. 846-852). IEEE. http://doi.org/10.1109/ICICT60155.2024.10545011

Susilo, T. (2024). The Role of Artificial Intelligence in Personalizing Learning for Each Student. JILTECH: Journal International of Lingua & Technology, 3(2). http://doi.org/10.55849/jiltech.v3i2.632

Subramanian, K. R. (2017). Product promotion in an era of shrinking attention span. International Journal of Engineering and Management Research (IJEMR), 7(2), 85-91.

Triansyah, F. A., Muhammad, I., Rabuandika, A., Siregar, K. D. P., Teapon, N., &Assabana, M. S. (2023). Bibliometric Analysis: Artificial Intelligence (AI) in High School Education. JurnalIlmiahPendidikan Dan Pembelajaran, 7(1), 112-123. http://doi.org/10.23887/jipp.v7i1.59718

Vetrivel, S. C., Vidhyapriya, P., &Arun, V. P. (2025). The Role of AI in Transforming Assessment Practices in Education. In AI Applications and Strategies in Teacher Education (pp. 43-70). IGI Global. http://doi.org/10.4018/979-8-3693-5443-8.ch003

Vargas-Murillo, A. R., de la Asuncion, I. N. M., & de Jesús Guevara-Soto, F. (2023). Challenges and opportunities of AI-assisted learning: A systematic literature review on the impact of ChatGPT usage in higher education. International Journal of Learning, Teaching and Educational Research, 22(7), 122-135. https://doi.org/10.26803/ijlter.22.7.7

Zaman, B. U. (2023). Transforming education through AI, benefits, risks, and ethical considerations. Authorea Preprints.

Zhu, Yunyi. (2024). The Impact of AI-Assisted Teaching on Students' Learning and Psychology. Journal of Education, Humanities and Social Sciences. 38. 111-116. http://doi.org/10.54097/k7a37d11

5

Smart Pedagogy: Harnessing AI for Financial Learning

Divya Khatwani
Research Scholar IILM University, Gurugram
Email: divya.khatwani.phd23@iilm.edu

Introduction

"AI won't replace teachers, but teachers who use AI will replace those who don't."
– Richard Culatta

This chapters explores how AI can transforms Financial Education through Innovative teaching Methodologies. Artificial Intelligence (AI) is revolutionizing various sectors at an unparalleled rate, and the field of education is no exception. The incorporation of AI within finance education offers a distinctive opportunity to augment the manner in which students comprehend financial principles, data analytics, and market dynamics. Through the utilization of AI, educators can develop tailored, interactive, and instantaneous learning experiences that equip students for the intricacies of the contemporary financial landscape.

The integration of artificial intelligence (AI) in teaching finance is a burgeoning field that offers innovative approaches to enhance financial literacy and education. AI systems, such as embodied social robots and virtual voice assistants, have been developed to teach financial literacy to young students, aiming to make learning more engaging and effective (Iqbal, 2023).

The accounting and finance sectors have historically embraced technological advancements — ranging from calculators and spreadsheets to the utilization of cloud computing. Nonetheless, the advent of generative artificial intelligence introduces both novel challenges and prospects for students aspiring to excel in the financial domain. Students may cultivate these competencies through formal coursework, professional certifications, and digital learning platforms. Andrew Harding, the chief executive of management accounting at the Association of International Certified Professional Accountants, underscores the significance of continuous professional development to maintain a competitive edge in a dynamic employment landscape: "Accounting and finance professionals must adjust their cognitive frameworks to learn, unlearn, and relearn," he asserts. (Murray, 2024)

The Evolution of Financial Education

Traditional finance education has historically depended on a combination of lectures, extensive textbooks, and theoretical case studies as its primary means of imparting knowledge to students who are eager to learn the intricacies of the field. Although these traditional methods have proven to be somewhat effective in teaching the fundamental concepts that underpin financial principles, they frequently fall short in their ability to accurately simulate the dynamic, fast-paced, and data-driven environment that characterizes the modern financial markets we see today. Furthermore, the rapid pace of change within the financial sector, which is largely fueled by groundbreaking innovations in technology such as artificial intelligence, big data analytics, and advanced machine learning techniques, has made these static teaching methods increasingly inadequate for preparing students for the realities of the industry. In order to cultivate practical skills and enhance adaptability, students must now actively engage with live data sets, participate in real-world scenarios, and interact with intelligent systems that challenge and refine their understanding of financial concepts.

Understanding Smart Pedagogy

Smart Pedagogy can be accurately characterized as a contemporary educational framework that is fundamentally driven by technological advancements, which prioritizes the creation of personalized, interactive, and adaptive learning experiences tailored to the individual needs of learners. This innovative approach harnesses the power of state-of-the-art technologies to address a wide array of diverse learning requirements, enhance student engagement through various interactive methodologies, and furnish educators and learners alike with immediate feedback that can significantly improve the educational process.

The principles that underpin smart pedagogy are multifaceted, with personalization being a core tenet: This particular aspect of smart pedagogy acknowledges the inherent uniqueness of each student, recognizing that individuals possess distinct learning preferences, styles, and paces that must be taken into account for effective educational outcomes. To facilitate this tailored approach, artificial intelligence (AI) tools, exemplified by adaptive learning platforms, are employed to meticulously customize educational content and assessments, thereby ensuring that the learning experience is both effective and specifically aligned with the individual needs of each student.

Interactivity is another essential component of smart pedagogy that plays a vital role in promoting student engagement and encouraging active participation in the learning process. Through the utilization of AI-powered simulations, immersive virtual reality (VR) experiences, and gamified educational tools, educational institutions are able to create remarkably immersive environments wherein students have the opportunity to apply their theoretical knowledge to practical scenarios, thereby reinforcing their understanding and retention of the subject matter.

Furthermore, the concept of real-time learning is integral to the framework of smart pedagogy, as it facilitates the integration of current information and feedback into the educational experience. Utilizing sophisticated AI systems enables the analysis of live market data, providing students with instant feedback regarding their performance while simultaneously allowing for the dynamic adjustment of their learning paths based on their ongoing progress and the current context of the subject being studied.

The core of smart pedagogy lies in its adaptability and personalization, allowing educational experiences to be tailored to individual learning styles and needs, thus enabling students to progress at their own pace and receive targeted support (Aggarwal et al., 2024).

The introduction and subsequent implementation of innovative and advanced technological systems within the educational sector not only provides an array of significant advantages but also contributes to the overall enhancement of the learning environment and pedagogical approaches.

Learners derive substantial benefits from engaging in educational experiences that utilize technology, as they often find enjoyment in the interactive elements it presents, and they are inherently predisposed to grasp the concepts and information conveyed by their educators, facilitated by the extensive availability of diverse educational resources.

The seamless integration of technology into the educational framework empowers individuals to actualize their inherent potential for creativity and effective learning, thereby fostering a more dynamic and engaging educational experience. Students exhibit a marked improvement in their learning outcomes when they employ technological tools and resources to deepen their understanding of the material presented by their instructors, leading to a more enriched and effective educational journey. (Dehbi et al., 2024)

Benefits of AI in Finance Education

The integration of AI in education systems is seen as a priority for economic growth, with significant investments in AI programs expected to increase accessibility to knowledge and improve educational quality (Osetskyi et al., 2020)

Artificial intelligence (AI) offers significant benefits in finance education, enhancing both financial literacy and economic stability across various demographics. AI-driven platforms can personalize financial education by using machine learning algorithms to identify individual knowledge gaps and provide tailored resources, making financial concepts more accessible and engaging through gamification and interactive tools (Opeyemi et al., 2024)

The integration of AI-powered educational tools significantly enhances the interactive nature of the learning experience, thereby creating a more immersive environment that ultimately fosters a higher level of engagement among students. For example, the implementation of gamified learning platforms, in conjunction with virtual trading simulations, cultivates dynamic and engaging environments that facilitate a deeper understanding of intricate financial concepts, which are often challenging for students to grasp.

Furthermore, the application of AI in educational contexts enables the development of personalized learning experiences, as it allows for the meticulous tailoring of content to meet the specific needs and progress of each individual student. This personalized approach is instrumental in ensuring that students attain a solid comprehension of foundational financial concepts prior to advancing to more complex topics, which in turn significantly enhances the overall learning outcomes for all participants involved.

Moreover, AI-driven simulations provide students with invaluable opportunities to acquire hands-on experience in various critical areas such as financial trading, portfolio management, and risk assessment, effectively bridging the often-cited gap that exists between theoretical knowledge and practical application in real-world scenarios.

In addition, the utilization of AI analytics equips educators with essential insights regarding student performance, thereby enabling them to pinpoint specific learning gaps and subsequently adapt their teaching methodologies in a more effective and responsive manner. This data-driven approach leads to instruction that is not only more targeted but also significantly more effective in addressing the diverse learning needs of students.

Cultivating familiarity with AI tools and methodologies is paramount in preparing students for successful careers within an increasingly automated financial industry. Through this exposure, students develop critical competencies in data analysis, machine learning, and decision-making processes, all of which are highly coveted by employers in today's competitive job market.

Additionally, AI-driven personalized financial coaching can empower women by providing customized financial advice, addressing barriers to financial literacy and promoting financial inclusion (Adelaja et al., 2024)

Applications of AI in Financial Learning

One of the most significant advantages that artificial intelligence brings to the educational sphere is its highly targeted and nuanced approach to the pedagogical process, which allows for a more individualized learning experience. In contrast, traditional classroom environments frequently encounter considerable difficulties when attempting to accommodate the wide array of diverse learning needs that students exhibit, leading to disparities in educational outcomes. Nevertheless, with the integration of artificial intelligence technologies, students are now afforded the opportunity to comprehend intricate and multifaceted concepts in a manner that is not only more effective but also allows them to progress at a pace that aligns with their unique learning trajectories.

The inherently adaptive characteristics of artificial intelligence algorithms facilitate the provision of customized instructional content to students, thereby ensuring that they achieve a comprehensive understanding of the subject matter before advancing to subsequent topics. This individualized pedagogical strategy has been empirically demonstrated to result in substantial improvements in both academic performance metrics and retention rates among learners, highlighting the efficacy of such an approach in contemporary educational practices.

Moreover, artificial intelligence possesses the remarkable potential to significantly enhance levels of student engagement and intrinsic motivation within the learning environment. For instance, virtual tutors that are powered by artificial intelligence technology are capable of interacting dynamically with students, delivering personalized feedback and guidance that resonates with each learner's specific educational needs and challenges.

An artificial intelligence-driven tutoring tool designed for students has the remarkable ability to modify its instructional techniques to align with the diverse individual learning styles and preferences that characterize the student population, thereby rendering the educational experience not only more engaging but also markedly more enjoyable for the learners involved in the process.

By seamlessly incorporating interactive elements such as gamification strategies and virtual reality applications, artificial intelligence can construct immersive learning experiences that not only capture the attention of students but also cultivate a profound passion for the pursuit of knowledge and lifelong learning.

Challenges Faced

Artificial intelligence platforms frequently engage in the collection of a vast array of personal information from students, encompassing their academic performance records, behavioral metrics, and demographic data. The potential risks associated with data breaches and the misuse of such sensitive information are considerable, necessitating that educational institutions implement rigorous and effective measures to safeguard this data, all while ensuring compliance with pertinent regulations.

The process of integrating artificial intelligence into educational frameworks can incur significant financial costs, necessitating substantial investments in various elements such as specialized software, advanced hardware, and comprehensive training programs. Furthermore, the constraints related to available resources might severely limit the accessibility of these AI tools, particularly for educational institutions that are situated in developing regions or for those that operate under tighter financial budgets.

Consequently, students may develop a dependency on AI solutions for their problem-solving needs, which could inhibit their ability to cultivate critical thinking and analytical skills that are vital for their overall intellectual development.

Instructors have the responsibility to not only elucidate the foundational concepts that underpin each financial calculation but also to incorporate a variety of conceptual inquiries within the assessments administered during the course examinations. In the unfortunate event that a student fails to grasp the underlying principles associated with a particular formula, the act of merely memorizing that formula may prove to be of limited utility and effectiveness. Furthermore, students are significantly more inclined to incorrectly apply a formula that they do not fully comprehend or understand, which can lead to erroneous conclusions and outcomes in their financial analysis. For instance, the artificial intelligence model known as ChatGPT is incapable of accurately determining the weighted average cost of capital (WACC) for a privately held company, primarily due to the fact that the requisite inputs needed to compute a privately held company's WACC are not easily accessible or obtainable in a straightforward manner; thus, qualitative judgment becomes essential in order to identify and select appropriate inputs for such calculations. (Steven Wasserman, 2023)

Conclusion

The amalgamation of artificial intelligence into finance education signifies a transformative shift that presents exceptional prospects for enhancing the educational experience and equipping students for the swiftly changing financial milieu. By utilizing AI methodologies such as machine learning, natural language processing, and sophisticated data analytics, educators can develop personalized, interactive, and adaptive educational frameworks. These frameworks not only promote a more profound comprehension of financial principles but also prepare students with the requisite practical competencies to thrive in a data-centric industry.

Although the advantages of artificial intelligence within finance education are substantial, encompassing heightened engagement, individualized instruction, and the cultivation of real-world skills, the implementation of this technology is accompanied by significant challenges. Concerns regarding data privacy, algorithmic bias, financial limitations, and the necessity for comprehensive educator training must be meticulously addressed. Furthermore, ethical considerations such as transparency, inclusiveness, and the judicious utilization of student data are critical to ensuring that AI functions as an equitable and efficacious instrument in the educational domain.

The effective assimilation of artificial intelligence in finance education relies on a judicious approach that harmonizes the capabilities of technology with the irreplaceable human dimension of teaching. By adopting this strategy, educators can empower students not only to comprehend and utilize AI but also to critically assess its applications and ramifications within the financial sector. As the discipline continues to advance, the incorporation of AI as a complement to conventional pedagogy will guarantee that finance education remains pertinent, impactful, and accessible in an increasingly intricate and automated landscape.

References

Aggarwal, D., Sharma, D., &Saxena, A. B. (2024). Smart Education: An Emerging Teaching Pedagogy for Interactive and Adaptive Learning Methods. *Journal of Learning and Educational Policy,44*, 1–9. https://doi.org/10.55529/jlep.44.1.9

Dehbi, A., Bakhouyi, A., Khaddar, A. M., &Talea, M. (2025). Education and smart technologies: towards a new pedagogical paradigm. *International Journal of Evaluation and Research in Education (IJERE), 14*(1), 297.https://doi.org/10.11591/ijere.v14i1.30470

Ferreira de Melo, E. (2023). Application of AI Agents in Enhancing Financial Education Games: A Case Study. *International Journal of Science and Research (IJSR), 12*(7), 1542–1551. https://doi.org/10.21275/SR23713234609

Komáromi, G. (2023). Designing Assignments for University Students in the Age of AI: Examples from Business Finance Education.*Journal of Education and Practice*.https://doi.org/10.7176/JEP/14-18-15

MOŞTEANU, N. R. (2022). Improving Quality of Online Teaching Finance and Business Management Using Artificial Intelligence and Backward Design.*Quality - Access to Success, 23*(187).https://doi.org/10.47750/QAS/23.187.01

Murray, S. (2024, June 16). AI in finance is like 'moving from typewriters to word processors.' *Financial Times*.

Yang, C., &Stivers, A. (2023). Investigating AI Languages' Ability to Solve Undergraduate Finance Problems.*SSRN Electronic Journal*.https://doi.org/10.2139/ssrn.4460814

Zhang, A., & Zhao, Y. (2022, October 27). Future Challenges of Accounting Education in China Using Artificial Intelligence Assisted Multimedia Based Smart Accounting System.*ACM Transactions on Asian and Low-Resource Language Information Processing*.https://doi.org/10.1145/3517914

https://www.forbes.com/sites/stevenwasserman/2023/08/13/how-ai-impacts-teaching-future-financial-leaders/

Adesola Oluwatosin Adelaja, Bibitayo Ebunlomo Abikoye, Michelle Chibogu Nezianya, Olamide Raimat Amosu, & Oluwatoyin Funmilayo Ayodele. (2024). Harnessing AI for personalized financial coaching: A pathway to financial inclusion and empowerment for women in the United States. *World Journal of Advanced Research and Reviews, 23*(2), 1356–1367. https://doi.org/10.30574/wjarr.2024.23.2.2491

Adeyelu Oluwatobi Opeyemi, Somto Emmanuel Ewim, Ngodoo Joy Sam-Bulya, &BulyaTolulopeOgundipe.(2024). Leveraging AI-Driven financial literacy and tax compliance solutions to foster economic growth in underserved communities and small businesses.*International Journal of Advanced Economics, 6*(10), 561–579. https://doi.org/10.51594/ijae.v6i10.1668

Amos Abidemi Ogunola, & Adriana N Dugbartey. (2024). AI-powered financial tools for student debt management in the U.S.: Enhancing financial literacy and economic stability. *World Journal of Advanced Research and Reviews, 24*(2), 868–891. https://doi.org/10.30574/wjarr.2024.24.2.3441

Dehbi, A., Bakhouyi, A., Khaddar, A. M., &Talea, M. (2025). Education and smart technologies: towards a new pedagogical paradigm. *International Journal of Evaluation and Research in Education (IJERE), 14*(1), 297.https://doi.org/10.11591/ijere.v14i1.30470

Dheepiga, S., &Sivakumar, N. (2024). *Exploring the Intersection of AI and Financial Literacy* (pp. 226–234). https://doi.org/10.4018/979-8-3693-5593-0.ch016

Ferreira de Melo, E. (2023). Application of AI Agents in Enhancing Financial Education Games: A Case Study. *International Journal of Science and Research (IJSR), 12*(7), 1542–1551. https://doi.org/10.21275/SR23713234609

Kakde, H., & Lad, K. (2024). Impact of Artificial Intelligence and Machine Learning Adoption in Finance.*Indian Journal of Computer Science, 9*(2), 8.https://doi.org/10.17010/ijcs/2024/v9/i2/173859

Kaur, M., &Dhiman, Dr. B. (2024). A Framework For Exploring The Integration Of AI And Financial Literacy Toward A Sustainable Financial Ecosystem. *Educational Administration: Theory and Practice.* https://doi.org/10.53555/kuey.v30i4.2382

Lakshmi, Y. (2024). THE IMPACT OF ARTIFICIAL INTELLIGENCE ON FINANCIAL LITERACY.*ShodhKosh: Journal of Visual and Performing Arts, 5*(5). https://doi.org/10.29121/shodhkosh.v5.i5.2024.1606

Manoharan, G., Nithya, G., Rajchandar, K., Razak, A., Gupta, S., Durai, S., &Ashtikar, S. P. (2024). *AI in Finance and Banking* (pp. 1–28).https://doi.org/10.4018/979-8-3693-2061-7.ch001

Miu, C., Gopurathingal, J., Thota, V., Thompson, M., van Beek, N., Kuczynski, J., Gadewadikar, J., &Iqbal, T. (2022). A Financial Literacy AI-Enabled Voice Assistant System for Educational Use.*2022 Systems and Information Engineering Design Symposium (SIEDS)*, 345–350. https://doi.org/10.1109/SIEDS55548.2022.9799370

Pillai, D., Singh, A. S., Bhosale, T., &Doifode, A. (2023). A Perspective on the Application of Fintech as a Gateway for Financial Literacy.*2023 International Conference on Information Technology (ICIT)*, 811–814. https://doi.org/10.1109/ICIT58056.2023.10225810

Rita Jain. (2023). Role of artificial intelligence in banking and finance.*Journal of Management and Science, 13*(3), 1–4. https://doi.org/10.26524/jms.13.27

Sattar, S., Latif, S., Ali Syed, A., &FaheemUllah, M. (2024). The Future of Finance Education in Pakistan: Preparing for an AI-Driven Industry. *Journal of Asian Development Studies, 13*(3), 1652–1659. https://doi.org/10.62345/jads.2024.13.3.133

Singh, R., Bansal, R., &Niranjanamurthy, M. (2023). Use and Application of Artificial Intelligence in Accounting and Finance.In *Data Wrangling* (pp. 251–274).Wiley.https://doi.org/10.1002/9781119879862.ch12

Surugiu, C., Gradinaru, C., &Surugiu, M.-R. (2024). Artificial Intelligence in Business Education: Benefits and Tools. *Amfiteatru Economic, 26*(65), 241.https://doi.org/10.24818/EA/2024/65/241

M., B., Dharmananda, M., M., M., Patel, S., Mohammed, M., &Reguraman, M. (2024). *Emerging Trends and Innovations of Artificial Intelligence in the Accounting and Financial Landscape* (pp. 575–598). https://doi.org/10.4018/979-8-3693-5380-6.ch023

Zaman, B. U. iu. (2024). *Transforming Education Through AI Benefits Risks and Ethical Considerations.* https://doi.org/10.20944/preprints202407.0859.v1

6

The Role of Human Resources in Fostering Effective Mediation and Negotiation Processes

Ms. Simran Kaur
IILM University Gurugram

Abstract

Because different people have different personalities, values, and working methods, therefore conflict in the workplace is unavoidable. Resolving conflicts effectively is essential to preserving a positive workplace culture and guaranteeing organizational success. Through the implementation of organized procedures, training, and the promotion of an open communication culture, human resources (HR) play an indispensable part in controlling and resolving conflicts. Any workplace will inevitably have conflict due to variations in viewpoints, personalities, and methods of operation. Unresolved disagreements frequently contribute to lower motivation, output, and employee retention, even if some conflicts can result in beneficial results like innovation and improved procedures. Human resources professionals play a crucial role in conflict resolution since they are responsible for making sure that disputes are handled in a way that promotes both employee well-being and corporate objectives. The methods and resources used by HR have a major impact on how well conflicts are resolved. These consist of formal dispute resolution procedures, conflict management training courses, and open lines of communication. Beyond mediation, HR's duty includes creating a culture that reduces conflict and promotes cooperation and understanding among staff members. The methods HR departments can use to manage disputes, the significance of conflict resolution for worker happiness and output, and the effects of unresolved disputes on organizational dynamics are all covered in this article.

Keywords: *Human Resources, Conflict Resolution, Workplace Conflict, Employee Relations, Organizational Culture, Communication Strategies, Mediation.*

1. Introduction

Destructive disputes are less likely to occur in a workplace that values diversity, inclusivity, and open communication.[1] By supporting team-building exercises, praising and rewarding cooperative efforts, and making sure that every employee feels valued and heard, HR can foster such a culture. After a dispute has been settled, HR should keep an eye on things to make sure the settlement is long-lasting and that no new problems crop up. Frequent follow-up may make the workplace more peaceful and stop disputes from happening again. Unresolved disputes may have detrimental effects on a company. They may result in high turnover rates, a poisonous workplace, and a decline in employee engagement. Furthermore, unresolved disputes frequently have detrimental impacts on team chemistry and overall productivity in addition to the persons directly engaged.[2] This emphasizes how crucial HR's proactive role in dispute resolution is.

1.1 Research Questions

- **Research Question-1:** How significant is the role of HR in promoting both employee well-being and corporate objectives?
- **Research Question-2:**How important is the role of HR in managing disputes and resolution of conflicts amongst employees in an organization?

2. HR as influencers of mediation and negotiation in organizations

According to mediators, there are two ways that mediation is used in organizations: either as a last-minute solution to a pressing conflict or as a gradual modification of policies to incorporate mediation as well as internal services, which could have been established by a mediation "champion" with

---

1 Mihalache M. & Mihalache, O.R.(2022).How workplace support for the COVID-19 pandemic and personality traits affect changes in employees' affective commitment to the organization and job- related well-being. *HRM61*(3) 295-314

2 Wilton, N., (2020). *An Introduction to Human Resource Management*(PHI)

clout within the company. By encouraging mediation more, HR professionals and mediators may help the little change spread across the company.[3]

HR professionals must first decide whether to incorporate negotiation and mediation into their policies and processes. Organizations have modified their protocols to incorporate mediation in cases when bullying or harassment accusations are made, and mediation is now a component of the dignity at work policies. Additionally, mediation is used to resolve litigation issues, return to work after a stress-related absence, protect disclosure (whistle-blowing), performance, a number of minor issues that have gone unresolved, interpersonal or general conflicts, and follow-up after the organization has addressed a complaint. In order for the parties to "get the work done," mediation may be requested in order to "rebuild work relations after an investigation."When there is dispute and the organization knows that its staff members are, in the terms of one mediator, "going nowhere," they also invite mediators to collaborate with them.4

3. HR practitioners as workplace mediators/negotiators

To facilitate referrals to mediation, mediators cultivate a social network of connections both inside and outside of organizations, usually through human resources professionals. HR professionals must choose which mediator or group of mediators is best to suggest to the parties to a certain conflict or disagreement. In order for internal issues to be referred to a mediator, professional to professional, the connection amongst workplace mediators and HR practitioners must be based on trust.[5]

The 21st century has seen a rise in the number of workplace mediators available to HR professionals. HR professionals may guarantee that mediators are qualified, certified, and experienced in order to give their company the greatest option for workplace mediators. Workplace mediation is frequently combined with many additional professional conflict engagement initiatives

3 Ahmad, S., Islam, T., Sadiq, M.&Kaleem, A. (2021).Promoting green behavior through ethical leadership: a model of green human resource management and environmental knowledge,*LODJ 42*(4) 531-547.

4 Dirani, K.M., Abadi, M., Alizadeh, A.&Barhate, B., (2020).Leadership competencies and the essential role of human resource development in times of crisis: a response to Covid-19 pandemic, *HRDI 23*(4) 380-394.

5 Elisa, Z.P., NabellaS.D.& Sari, D.P. (2022). The Influence of Role Perception, Human Resource Development, and Compensation on Employee Performance,*EJM 12*(3) 1606-1612.

by "general practitioners." The usage of mediation has changed throughout time, moving from mostly employer along with trade union labor to more individual or group difficulties. As a result, mediators are now situationally adaptable in the issues they handle. In addition, mediators create and carry out a mediation process according to the concerns and objectives of the parties involved.[6]Mediators find that a large portion of their employment originates from referrals and word-of-mouth, and HR professionals frequently discuss their experiences with mediators with other HR professionals. When mediation has worked for an organization in the past, they are more likely to invite the mediator to return or utilize mediation once again. Some mediators discover that they are sent to other cases from the same region after witnessing it work in circumstances when others believed it would not.

4. Operational efficacy of mediation

Depending on the concerns, the mediation process might take several forms. Understanding the process's components, how they may support the suggested process design, and what the organization must understand in terms of feedback is crucial for the HR practitioner in reaching an educated choice. The larger important question is how HR departments assess workplace mediation in order to guide future choices. This includes the information they have on file to help them make judgments about the costs of conflict and its resolution, alongside the effects of both on output, performance, and employee well-being at work.[7]The "three-stage mediation process" described in the literature is more frequently a "six-stage" procedure in practice as workplace mediation has developed to cover more individual conflict situations inside organizations. Additionally, one in four workplace negotiators have more enduring connections with HR professionals, with whom they collaborate to impact changes in workplaces or enhance conflict resolution abilities.

6 Hamouche, S.(2023).Human resource management and the COVID-19 crisis: Implications, challenges, opportunities, and future organizational directions, *JMO29*(5) 799-814.

7 Kilag, O.K., Largo, J.&Rabillas, A. (2024).Administrators' Conflict Management and Strategies,*IMJRISE* 1(1) 60-67.

8 Mahapatro, B. (2021). *Human resource management* (New Age International (P) ltd).

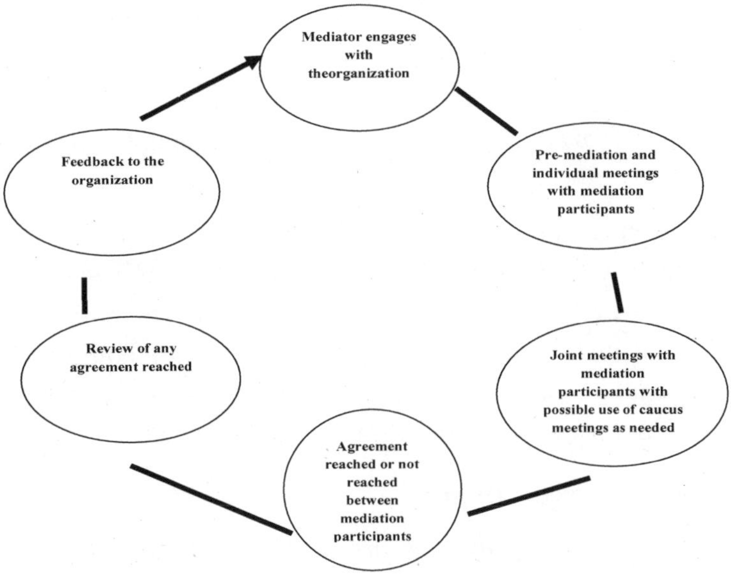

Figure: Six stages of workplace mediation[8]

5. Key components of an effective mediation process

Concerns with claimed harassment or discriminatory conduct in the workplace can be addressed through a variety of dispute resolution procedures. The individual who files a complaint frequently only wants to make sure that the improper action will cease and that others won't experience the same treatment. A conflict resolution procedure that provides chances for greater comprehension and solution bargaining could be necessary to get this kind of result. Negotiation is the process by which parties or representatives of those parties identify, exchange, reject, or accept ideas or proposals in order to reach mutually agreeable results. It might involve any kind of direct or indirect communication in which parties with conflicting interests discuss the type of collaborative action they might take to cope with and eventually settle their disagreements without the need for arbitration or a trial.[9]

Interest-based styles are at one end of a continuum that represents the wide range of negotiation procedures, while power-based styles are at the other end. In order to obtain one-sided advantages, a power-based negotiating

9 Mahapatro, B. (2021). *Human resource management* (New Age International (P) ltd).

10 Serit, A. (1992). Law Society of Upper Canada Research and Planning Committee, *SGDRT.*

approach usually entails power battles, strength statements, or power manipulation. The idea that "I win/you lose" is at the center of power-based bargaining. The idea that there is a defined or restricted quantity of resources or assets available for distribution is fundamental to power-based agreements.[10]

Generally speaking, power-based negotiating is inappropriate in the workplace since it causes individuals to quickly solidify in rigid, hostile attitudes. In most situations of harassment and discrimination, there has been a misuse of authority. A negotiating procedure based on power is likely to perpetuate that unfairness and further harm the individual or people who are the targets of the improper or illegal actions.

5.1 Interest-based negotiation

In situations when interests diverge, the interest-based or ethical negotiating approach enables all parties to concentrate on a resolution that is founded on an impartial and equitable standard while also seeking out opportunities for mutual advantage wherever feasible. Without making the other party feel taken advantage of, this kind of negotiating fosters an environment that helps all parties satisfy some or all of their wants and needs. Interest-based negotiations are therefore sometimes referred to as win-win. The emphasis is on using creativity to expand the parties' options, assets, solutions, and resources in terms of quantity and kind.

Employers, respondents, and complainants who are involved in settling workplace complaints frequently see an interest-based negotiating process favorably if it raises awareness of the detrimental effects of inappropriate actions and enables individuals to find solutions that are focused on the future. Experience has shown that few complainants choose to initiate a formal complaint or an internal inquiry. A procedure that enables people to voice their concerns without turning the complaint into the adversarial dispute is preferred by many complainants.[11]

In order to fulfill their legal responsibilities to the complaining party, the respondent, and other people, like coworkers or customers, who might be

---

11 Fischer R.&Ury, W. (2011).*Getting to Yes: Negotiating Agreement Without Giving In* (Penguin Books, 2nd ed.).

12 Forsythe, G.H. (2011). A Comparative Analysis of Canadian and American Law Relating to the Preservation of the Confidentiality of Settlement and Mediation Discussions.ProQuest.

impacted by the alleged behaviors that serve as the basis for the complaint, employers should keep this factor in mind and carefully evaluate, in conjunction with the organization's attorney, a variety of mediation and arbitration options. Compared to an inquiry or a formal complaint, a mediation procedure based on an interest-based negotiating paradigm may cause less disruption to the workplace. Additionally, it can offer the perfect setting for people to acquire new, more respectable habits while preserving their dignity.

Participants distance themselves from the issue, which is one of the traits of the interest-based negotiating process. For instance, instead of calling the offending individual a "racist" or a "harasser," participants talk about why an undesirable conduct has a bad effect. The participants were able to agree on desirable actions and their beneficial effects on coworkers and each other as a result of this conversation.

People benefit from the interest-based negotiating mediation process in the workplace since it:

- Promotes awareness-building and acceptance rather than negativity;
- Encourages independent and imaginative thinking rather than stiffness and traditional responses;
- Fosters an environment where people try to generate several possibilities and solutions;
- Promotes the use of impartial standards based on actuality, rather than subjective ideas founded on untested assumptions;
- Facilitates people to recognize and zero in on their needs rather than their "positions" or demands;
- Moves people from expressing their "power" to working together on innovative approaches that meet the present and projected requirements of all stakeholders;
- Encourages them to determine their BATNA.[12] It is possible to think of the best alternative to a negotiated agreement as the benchmark by which all negotiated agreements should be evaluated. If the negotiating process fails to provide a solution, the individual's BATNA can be determined by taking into account the options or opportunities

---

13 Best Alternative to a Negotiated Agreement

that the individual may exercise. The question, "If I decline to embrace the solution(s) suggested, what are my other options?" is frequently helpful while thinking about one's BATNA and "Will those alternative options satisfy my needs as well as the suggested solution or solutions?"

- Fosters preservation of working relationships rather than alienation and can result in improved workplace management strategies and other unexpected benefits that increase productivity and enhanced performance.

One might argue that the interest-based bargaining method is detrimental as it necessitates:[13]

- Enough tolerance and time to better comprehend underlying demands and spot any covert agendas
- Information sharing; innovative, fresh perspectives on other people; acceptance of (but not necessarily agreement therewith) the viewpoint of others;
- Confidence that information supplied won't be misused against one's interests; and readiness to determine one's BATNA

5.2 Effective communication skills

To help the participants concentrate on what they want and need (rather than their "positions") and communicate effectively with one another, the mediator must employ active listening techniques, a variety of questioning techniques, and acknowledgement during the interest-based negotiation process. Among the abilities needed for effective communication are:[14]

Reframing:A participant's negative comment is restated by the mediator with an optimistic, forward-looking goal. When one party tells another, "You always disappoint me," for instance, the mediator might rephrase this to say, "You need the other person to show that you can follow through on promises in order to reach an agreement." Through reframing, people can shift their attention from their unfavorable opinions of the other person to the wants or interests that need to be satisfied.

14 Kilag, O.K., Largo, J.&Rabillas, A. (2024).Administrators' Conflict Management and Strategies, *IMJRISE* 1(1) 60-67.

15 BollenK.&Euwema, M. (2013).State of the Art, Workplace Mediation: An Underdeveloped Research Area, *NJ*29 (3) 329–53.

Refocusing: Before someone says something unpleasant, the mediator steps in and asks them to rephrase the good aspect of their statement. For instance, if one participant tells another: I appreciate it when you show these positive behaviors, but you are cruel because you always..., the mediator can interrupt before the negatives are listed and ask a follow-up question to get the participant to elaborate on the positive behaviors.

Clarifying: By posing a question, the mediator elicits further details and comprehension from the participant. For instance: Could you explain your statement that you feel uneasy when ...?

Using open-ended questioning: The mediator asks the participant to elaborate on any underlying details, significance, or ideals that the speaker finds significant. For instance: What is it about such admirable actions that give you a sense of respect? Applying the principle of consequential inquiry: By posing questions that ask participants to consider the long-term effects of their proposed solutions, the mediator helps them to consider their requirements, for instance: How would your recommendation that this supervisor be dismissed help the objective of persuading other supervisors to agree that positive conduct boosts employee morale? The mediator might encourage the participants to perform a reality check by posing meaningful questions.

These are just a handful of the numerous efficient communication strategies that managers and staff might acquire. These communication strategies are commonly employed by mediators to help participants settle accusations of harassment at work. They can also be very important parts of the daily skill sets that can greatly improve employees' capacity to communicate with coworkers and others who do deal with your company.

6. Overview of the mediation process

The mediators that are available to oversee the mediation process determine how flexible the procedure is. The following concurrent actions are likely to be taken by a mediator in a workplace dispute including claims of harassment and discrimination:[15]

- Hold separate pre-mediation sessions to collect information with all of the important parties, including the employer's representative, the individual who is allegedly involved in the conduct, the person who

16 Brubaker, D., Noble, C., Fincher, R.&Park S.K.Y. (2014). Conflict resolution in the workplace: what will the future bring?,*CRQ*31(4) 357–86.

is worried about the behaviors, and the supervisor or supervisors of each of these persons. At this point, the mediator's duties include assisting the parties in comprehending the mediation procedure, gathering data, identifying problems, resolving power disparities, and identifying and resolving process difficulties.

- Help the participants reach a consensus, ideally in writing, about the purpose of the procedure, the regulations or rules that will be adhered to, and the expected degree of secrecy.

Following the completion of the aforementioned, the mediator will determine if it is physically and emotionally safe for the people involved to meet either immediately or indirectly after consulting with the participants. The next step of the procedure may be conducted by the mediator meeting with all or some of the participants. The parties get the chance to meet in person and engage in more direct communication at this phase of the mediation process. In order to provide participants some solitude during the process and to relieve the physical and mental stress of face-to-face interactions, breakout rooms could be offered.

If the participants are physically or emotionally uncomfortable together, the mediator might prefer to serve as a "go-between" or shuttle diplomat. To maintain the parties physically secured, the mediator could also advise the parties to employ technology like speaker phones or video conferencing. The following guidelines and procedures are likely to be included in this interactive portion of the mediation process:[16]

- The mediator will make an opening remark to start the mediation session. The opening statement aims to provide an overview of the following: the responsibilities of the mediator and participants; the process's goal; the benefits of using mediation to resolve issues; the dangers of not using mediation to resolve issues; confidentiality safeguards; and acceptable process expectations. The mediator will probably ask the parties to establish fundamental regulations and confidentiality agreements at this point in the process. After that, the mediator will determine the broad scope of the problems and try to reach an agreement on a conversation agenda.
- The individual who is worried about the behavior may be asked to

17 Kenny, T.(2014).Developing the conversation about workplace mediation, *JMACA*1(1).

describe how they see the behaviors in issue. The person could also be asked to explain how the actions or incidents affected them. At this point, certain emotional outbursts could happen.

- The individual answering the questions will be asked to describe how they view the actions or occurrences. At this point, it may be possible to identify the requirements of this person that require attention. There may also be some emotional outbursts.
- Additional stakeholders, including a manager, supervisor, or union representative, could also be invited to take part and provide their perspectives, especially about the systemic problems at hand and how the issues affect other workers and the company.
- The mediator may rephrase, explain, and ask each participant for further information in between the aforementioned phases. Either all of the participants or only one person may be present during this procedure. In this stage, the mediator will try to determine the participants' needs and goals, both individual and shared, as well as any systemic or associated problems that require attention.

7. Conclusion

Human resources play a complex and vital role in dispute resolution for the well-being of any firm. HR may successfully handle disagreements by creating clear protocols, offering training, and cultivating a healthy workplace culture, transforming possible setbacks into chances for development and cooperation. It is impossible to overestimate the significance of HR's involvement in dispute resolution since it has a direct bearing on long-term success, organizational productivity, and employee happiness.

Bibliography

Ahmad, S., Islam, T., Sadiq, M. &Kaleem, A. (2021). Promoting green behavior through ethical leadership: a model of green human resource management and environmental knowledge, LODJ 42(4) 531-547.

Best Alternative to a Negotiated Agreement

Bollen K. &Euwema, M. (2013). State of the Art, Workplace Mediation: An Underdeveloped Research Area, NJ 29 (3) 329–53.

Bollen, K. and Euwema, M. (2013) State of the art, workplace mediation: an underdeveloped research area. Negotiation Journal. Vol 29, No 3. pp329–53.

Brubaker, D., Noble, C., Fincher, R. & Park S.K.Y. (2014). Conflict resolution in the workplace: what will the future bring?, CRQ 31(4) 357–86.

Brubaker, D., Noble, C., Fincher, R., Park, S. K.-Y. and Press, S. (2014) Conflict resolution in the workplace: what will the future bring? Conflict Resolution Quarterly. Vol 31, No 4. pp357–86.

Dirani, K.M., Abadi, M., Alizadeh, A. &Barhate, B., (2020). Leadership competencies and the essential role of human resource development in times of crisis: a response to Covid-19 pandemic, HRDI 23(4) 380-394.

Elisa, Z.P., Nabella S.D. & Sari, D.P. (2022). The Influence of Role Perception, Human Resource Development, and Compensation on Employee Performance, EJM 12(3) 1606-1612.

Fischer R. &Ury, W. (2011). Getting to Yes: Negotiating Agreement Without Giving In (Penguin Books, 2nd ed.).

Forsythe, G.H. (2011). A Comparative Analysis of Canadian and American Law Relating to the Preservation of the Confidentiality of Settlement and Mediation Discussions. ProQuest.

Hamouche, S. (2023). Human resource management and the COVID-19 crisis: Implications, challenges, opportunities, and future organizational directions, JMO 29(5) 799-814.

Kenny, T. (2014) Developing the conversation about workplace mediation. Journal of Mediation and Applied Conflict Analysis. Vol 1, No 1.

Kenny, T. (2014). Developing the conversation about workplace mediation, JMACA 1(1).

Kilag, O.K., Largo, J. &Rabillas, A. (2024). Administrators' Conflict Management and Strategies, IMJRISE 1(1) 60-67.

Kilag, O.K., Largo, J. &Rabillas, A. (2024). Administrators' Conflict Management and Strategies, IMJRISE 1(1) 60-67.

Kilag, O.K., Largo, J. &Rabillas, A. (2024). Administrators' Conflict Management and Strategies, IMJRISE 1(1) 60-67.

Law Reform Commission. (2010) Report on alternative dispute resolution: conciliation and mediation. Law Reform Commission of Ireland (LRC 98-2010).

Mahapatro, B. (2021). Human resource management (New Age International (P) ltd).

Mihalache M. &Mihalache, O.R. (2022). How workplace support for the COVID-19 pandemic and personality traits affect changes in employees' affective commitment to the organization and job- related well-being. HRM 61(3) 295-314.

Mihalache M. &Mihalache, O.R. (2022). How workplace support for the COVID-19 pandemic and personality traits affect changes in employees' affective commitment to the organization and job- related well-being. HRM 61(3) 295-314.

Serit, A. (1992). Law Society of Upper Canada Research and Planning Committee, SGDRT.

Teague, P., Roche, W. and Hann, D. (2012) The diffusion of alternative dispute resolution practices in Ireland. Economic and Industrial Democracy. Vol 33, No 4. pp581–604.

Teague, P., Roche, W. and Hann, D. (2012) The diffusion of alternative dispute resolution practices in Ireland. Economic and Industrial Democracy. Vol 33, No 4. pp581–604.

Wilton, N., (2020). An Introduction to Human Resource Management (PHI)